MAXIMIZING
CASH FLOW

Small Business Management Series
Rick Stephan Hayes, Editor

MAXIMIZING CASH FLOW

Practical Financial Controls
for Your Business

Emery Toncré

JOHN WILEY & SONS
New York • Chichester • Brisbane • Toronto • Singapore

Library of Congress Cataloging in Publication Data:

Toncré, Emery
  Maximizing cash flow.

  (Wiley series on small business management)
  1. Cash management.   2. Cash flow.   I. Title.
II. Series.

HG4028.C45T66 1986   658.1'5244   85-29643
ISBN 0-471-80744-3

Printed in the United States of America

10 9 8 7 6 5 4 3 2 1

To Lois Jean, my wife,
    for her understanding and encouragement

        and

Erich and Marc, my two sons,
    for their youthful enthusiasm to show me the way

        and

Mandy, our family Airedale,
    who never left my side during the entire effort

PREFACE

Of all the causes of business failure, the mismanagement of cash ranks near the top. Cash is commonly referred to as "the bottom line," and for good reason: a sudden cash deficiency can quickly turn a profitable operation into a losing venture. To complicate matters further, cash problems are usually misunderstood and ignored by many business owners, who leave them to the accountant to resolve. Leaving cash and related problems to professionals may be prudent in some cases, but it circumvents the business owner's opportunity to understand the basic problems resulting from cash shortages. Without such an understanding, business owners can find themselves in a difficult position, because the majority of business problems today can be traced to poor cash management.

For example, cash shortages can result in purchasing less resale inventory which, in turn, can cause a loss of customers and an eventual drop in total sales volume. A shortage in cash can delay payments of outstanding invoices, which will inevitably raise questions about the owner's credit. Perhaps the most serious consequence is the restrictions cash shortages can place on a business owner's actions. Without available funds the owner cannot afford to expand, buy new equipment, or hire additional people even though business projections may warrant expansion. Finally, nothing can be more disturbing to a business owner striving to build and ensure a future than to have to turn away business because of insufficient working capital.

Given the enormous impact cash has on business activities, you might ask why cash problems are not resolved before a business experiences a shortage. The answer is simple. *The average business owner does not know how to control his cash funds.* It is easy to understand how cash affects available cash reserves or listen to an accountant's warnings about what the lack of cash is doing to your current financial position, but it is not so easy to know what to do about it. As a business owner, do you know how to establish a control over your cash funds in order to sustain a reasonable level of working capital? If not, this book is intended for you.

EMERY TONCRÉ

Convent Station, New Jersey
March 1986

CONTENTS

MAXIMIZING
CASH FLOW

1

FROM MISCONCEPTION TO INDIFFERENCE

By definition, cash serves as legal tender in the exchange of value for products and services between individuals and businesses. For a business owner, cash is the bottom line by which day-to-day operations are conducted. Practically speaking, there are no business actions an owner can take that do not in some way affect the available cash of the operation. And although a business owner may jokingly refer to cash as something everyone else has, what he is alluding to is the problem of maintaining acceptable levels of cash reserves for business operations. Given the fact that cash is the ultimate measure of success and survival, the sobering fact is that many business owners today do not understand the purpose or role cash plays in their businesses or the steps that are available to them to acquire additional funds, leading to an attitude of indifference. Let's examine each of these points more carefully.

LACK OF UNDERSTANDING

The lack of cash, resulting from poor cash management and control by business owners who do not understand the role

1

cash plays in business, has led many to certain failure. Over
the past few years, 9 out of every 10 business owners have
become victims of the cash consequences of poor decision
making and of operating without sufficient levels of cash
reserves. Despite this strong correlation between business
failure and the need for cash, cash problems are usually
misunderstood and ignored by many business owners and
left for an accountant to resolve, although the consequences
are dear. For example, a shortage in cash can delay the payment of outstanding invoices, thereby raising unwarranted
questions about the owner's credit. But questions with respect to the owner's credit are not as serious as restrictions
placed on the owner's actions resulting from the lack of cash.
Without sufficient operating funds, commonly referred to as
working capital, the owner cannot afford to expand, buy new
equipment, or hire additional people, even though business
projections may warrant expansion. Nothing can be more
disturbing to a business owner striving to build and ensure
a future than to have to turn away business because he or
she lacks the necessary cash to cover day-to-day operations
and still provide for reasonable expansion.

Given the enormous impact cash has on business activities, it is reasonable to ask why cash problems can't be resolved before it is too late. *The simple fact is that the average
business owner does not know how to control working capital because he or she does not understand how cash reserves
become depleted or what to do to restore additional funds.*

Some business actions can deplete working capital while
the company is still generating profits. Drawing money from
the business for personal use, for example, reduces cash
funds but has no effect on profits because it is not considered
an expense item normally deducted from profits. Many
business owners find this difficult to understand, given the
widely accepted correlation between cash and profits. This
misunderstanding of the effect cash disbursements have on
taxable profits has caused more than one business to fail.

Let's review some other examples of cash disbursements
where the effects on cash reserves and profit vary.

Company Debts

The most well-recognized cash disbursement is the payment of a company debt, either short- or long-term. Today, the rate of interest for most company loans is usually one or two points over the current prime rate (the interest rate charged by banks on loans to their best customers). The principal amount of the loan, which is a balance sheet disbursement, will always remain constant, but the interest expense that is part of the total payment is a deductible profit and loss item which will vary from month to month. Thus, cash reserves are reduced by the total payout, but only the interest portion affects profits.

Cash Disbursements for Investment Purposes

In an effort to make money on money, many business owners invest idle cash in various investment programs. This makes good sense as long as a balance is maintained between short-term investments, which return a lower rate but offer easy accessibility to the money, and longer-term investments, which pay higher interest rates but require that the investment remain intact over longer periods of time. The amount of the short-term investment should be governed by the company's need for cash to meet continuing costs that do not change with increased business activity and emergency needs. In either case, cash profits can be increased by this disbursement if the investment is sound.

Acquisition of Capital Equipment

Companies that buy capital equipment, such as machinery, can either pay for the item in full or make a downpayment and pay the balance over an agreed-on period of time, plus interest. Some equipment can be leased with an option to buy—a plan often adopted to conserve cash reserves. Available cash-on-hand along with projected cash needs generally dictate which course of action a business will choose. Although working capital is reduced by the cost of any equipment regardless of how the equipment is acquired, profits are affected only when the equipment is leased, the interest payment made for the loan, and the amount of depreciation allowed each year.

Acquisition of Real Property

Many business owners find it profitable to own the building in which the business conducts operations. Other owners have gone a step further, becoming landlords and leasing a portion of the premises to other businesses. There are pluses and minuses to these actions. Certainly, owning your own building eliminates the expense of a lease. But becoming a landlord increases your costs of maintaining the premises. Business owners who are both landlords and operators usually justify their actions by pointing to the fact that their buildings can be depreciated as expense deductions, which decreases profits subject to taxes, while their market value increases with inflation. There is much to be said in favor of this point of view so long as real estate property continues to increase in value. But if the economy weakens to the extent that commercial real estate property drops in value, a business owner could find him- or herself with committed cash reserves and a piece of unsalable property. Either way, working capital will be depleted while the profitability of this action remains questionable.

Leasehold Improvements

Business owners who lease or own their own buildings always need cash disbursements to improve facilities as a way of improving productivity. If the improvements increase efficiency, the additional cost can usually be justified. However, leasehold improvements that have no purpose but to give the existing facility a facelift should be considered excessive expenditures that place an undue drain on cash reserves without discernible return on investment. In such a case, all disbursement for improvements will reduce available working capital funds with a deferred effect on reducing profits as the improvements are written off over a specific number of years.

Shareholders' Loans

Quite often, sharehold loans will be granted on highly favorable terms. Generally, this practice is justified on the basis that a shareholder has a better justification for the need of the additional money. Of course, this is true, but the owner/operator should determine before making such a loan whether it is being done at the expense of other shareholders. Since this is a total drain on cash reserves, an owner must remember that the needs of the corporation come first and that shareholders' loans should be based on good business reasons rather than good shareholder relations.

ACQUISITION OF ADDITIONAL FUNDS

Along with having only a vague understanding of the connection between cash and profits, small business owners are notorious for starting new businesses without sufficient working capital. A few years ago, when a small business just starting suffered from the usual lack of sufficient working capital, many frugal business owners were able to overcome their cash problems. But today business owners are also faced with problems of collecting money on time, and they are often forced to hold payment from their own vendors until they have been paid, further compounding the cash problem. Under today's conditions of tight money, this inability to collect receivables and lack of money to pay vendors has made everyone, regardless of number of years in business, face the same problem—lack of cash. Thus, this problem is no longer simply one of insufficient working capital in the initial stages; what we have now is a national epidemic of cash-poor businesses becoming candidates for failure.

Most business owners know by instinct or by simply looking at the current balance in their checkbooks whether or not their cash needs are serious. *What they fail to understand is the simple fact that steps can be taken to acquire additional funds to meet their needs.*

Additional cash can come from many sources. The most common source is income, which will be discussed later in more detail, but there are other sources of cash that are not so obvious. Let's examine some of these sources of funds.

Accounts Receivable and Accounts Payable

Currently, the average business owner is finding that the ability to collect outstanding receivables is more difficult than finding markets for services or products. All of this has led to a practice that has closed the loop to a vicious circle: in order to maintain sufficient cash-funds, most business owners pay creditors only after being paid by their own customers! It has become a game in which everyone knows but no one will admit how tight cash reserves have become.

Many owners place delinquent accounts receivable with collection agencies, but these businesses have become so swamped with work that they generally attempt to collect only the most likely receivables. If an outstanding receivable is sufficient enough to warrant legal action, the business owner can place the uncollectible receivable in the hands of an attorney who will assess a sizeable fee on the amount eventually collected.

The answer to this dilemma is to establish a cash program for collecting accounts receivable and paying accounts payable. A cash-control program for accounts receivable should adopt the following rules:

Give no credit to any customer who has a poor record of performance in paying bills.

Arrange an agreement with slow-paying customers to pre-pay 25 to 33 percent of the total invoice in advance in order to cover your fixed expenses. As a trade-off for this prepayment, the remaining balance would then be due later than the normal billing time.

Be reasonable with your customers regarding cash collections.

Don't let your collection of accounts receivable be your only source of cash to maintain your working-capital level.

Govern accounts payable by an expense-control system, anticipating expenditures before they are incurred. Having this type of control built into your overall cash projection will ensure that sufficient working capital is available to cover expected expenditures.

Sometimes insufficient cash can lead to business failure if the problem is not resolved. In a recent text on how to avoid business bankruptcy (which I authored) I described in considerable detail other sources of acquiring cash. Let us review some of these additional action steps that can be initiated.

Banking relations. At a time when sufficient cash reserves are at a premium, it is good policy to maintain a close rapport with your banker. This should include quarterly financial statements and borrowing some money, enough for your needs but in line with your ability to pay, in order to establish a continual line of credit history with the bank. Banks are in business to loan money, and by keeping your banking relationships healthy you will help ensure that there will never be any question regarding a future request by you for additional funds. Short-term notes from the bank can provide you with additional money without having to drain your existing cash reserves. Under a good banking relationship, owners can actually extend the amount of total working capital by adding to available funds the additional funds from the bank in the case of emergency.

Inventory control. Another source of cash comes in the form of your ability to turn over inventory as often as possible. High inventory levels or slow turnovers have the effect of holding available cash in inventory, thereby reducing the amount of working capital funds that could be used for other needs. Your approach to controlling inventory will be the result of interfacing several factors, such as purchasing the proper amount of inventory at reasonable prices, choosing items that are salable, maintaining a control over the existing inventory levels for turnover purposes, moving obsolete inventory through sales promotions or similar techniques, and maintaining diversification in the variety of items on hand.

The proper amount of inventory depends upon expected sales, the lead time from order to delivery, and the physical space that is available for display or storage. The correlation between sales and inventory purchases should be maintained as a permanent management tool to determine the total inventory needed at any given point in time. However, it is impossible for a sales correlation to determine inventory levels item by item. So, to overcome this problem, inventory can be classified according to its costs and to the amount actually on hand. This control, referred to as the ABC method, places a greater control over the A items, which are more costly but fewer in number, and less control over the C items, which are relatively inexpensive per item and plentiful in number.

The lead time from order to delivery varies from vendor to vendor and item by item. It is an important factor to consider, because you must keep your shelves filled at all times and your storage inventory plentiful in order to maintain an effective marketing program. Empty display cases convey to customers the impression that you might be operating your business on a shoestring. And since sales impression is often the dominant factor in selling, a well-displayed and well-stocked shelf is vital. Additionally, it would be helpful if you kept records of the delivery time for each vendor. From these records you will be able to plan your orders in sufficient time to allow for delivery and provide adequate space.

The price you pay for resale items must be constantly reviewed. With the advent of creeping inflation, business owners everywhere, including your vendors, are constantly adjusting prices, generally upward, in order to sustain reasonable gross profits. From your standpoint, cash can be conserved by maintaining price records as well as delivery records on every vendor. Using these records, you can adjust your prices in accordance with vendor changes. In the meantime, it behooves you to initiate a program of comparative shopping to ascertain if you are getting the best products at the best possible price.

Choosing inventory items that will sell depends upon how good a merchandiser you are. Buying resale items always carries some element of risk, but an experienced businessperson who knows and understands his or her products has an instinct about what will sell and what won't sell. A simple rule to follow is to keep aware of new marketing trends that offer you the opportunity to diversify your salable items.

Maintaining accurate and updated records on physical inventory enables you to spot obsolete inventory before it becomes a cash problem. Obsolete inventory that fails to move restricts cash if not sold within a reasonable period of time. It can even mean a loss in profits. So, once an inventory item is obsolete, it should be offered as a sale item and moved from the shelves as quickly as possible. It is not only costly to keep obsolete inventory on hand, the product takes up needed space that could be used for fresh merchandise. Many business owners have been reluctant to sell obsolete merchandise by taking a reduction in price, but with today's tight cash problems, the quicker you dispose of these goods—even though the price may be below your initial cost—the stronger your working capital position will be for your future needs.

Shareholders' investment. For those business owners who are incorporated, additional funds can be acquired by selling additional shares of stock to existing shareholders or to new shareholders. At least three problems generally arise from this kind of action: the price to ask per share, the possibility of diluting the controlling interest of your corporation, and the problem of new shareholders who now must be treated with the same care as your original shareholders.

The selling price can be established in many different ways, the most common being book value plus value added for past and anticipated performance. Of course, as a business owner who wishes to sell additional shares you will find it to your advantage to present sufficient financial documentation to support a reasonably high price per share. Financial statements prepared by an accounting professional that demonstrate a record of acceptable performance, coupled with cash projections that show good growth potential, are generally sufficient to submit to a prospective shareholder. In closed corporations, where all stock is held by a select few individuals, a new issue of stock represents a good prospect for investors who wish to acquire more stock in a company especially if there is a good chance that the corporation is going public. Going public can make any stock attractive if it should increase its present value three to five times.

Of course, having additional shareholders means that there will be new faces in the corporation who will ask questions. However, it's doubtful that your existing control will be greatly diluted unless the additional shareholders are grouped together to prevent action on your part. To stop this from happening, an owner must be sure that the controlling shares are greater in number than the combined shares of all the minority stockholders.

Finally, it is often good policy to attempt to attract new shareholders who can bring newer concepts and expertise to your company. This is why you will find many professionals from related accounting, consulting and banking fields serving as minority shareholders and members of the boards of different companies. Selling stock will provide an additional source of cash, but an owner must be cautious to guard his or her equity position at all times.*

INDIFFERENCE

The problem with most business owners today is that they don't realize a problem actually exists until it becomes a crisis. If business owners would simply turn to a qualified financial professional for a total assessment of their cash needs, immediate steps could be taken in most cases to remedy a problem before it reaches this point. However, many business owners believe that their present accounting records contain enough detail to keep them informed of cash needs. Unfortunately they are usually wrong. It is widely accepted by most professionals that only one out of every four business owners takes the trouble to review accounting records carefully, and less than five percent of these have any knowledge of their present cash position or changes in cash flow over a prior period. Moreover, less than two percent of these have ever requested a cash projection and, therefore, are unable to make any business judgments regarding immediate cash needs or the future requirements for cash reserves. This lack of action on the part of most business owners is not the result of attempting to comprehend but failing to understand complex financial data; it arises from an attitude of total indifference to the need for *control over cash flow.* Admittedly, some professionals have done little to change the attitudes of business owners regarding cash flow, and many professionals have even gone so far as to stop reporting changes in cash flow because of the general indifference shown by business owners to the problem.

There is no doubt that accounting records and financial

*Excerpted, with permission, from Emery Toncré, *The Action-Step Plan to Avoiding Business Bankruptcy* (Englewood Cliffs, N.J.: Prentice-Hall, 1984), pp. 60–73.

statements can be difficult to understand for the average business owner. No one is suggesting that business owners tackle every aspect of the complex world of finance, along with their many other duties. But totally ignoring the problem of cash, hoping that it will disappear, is no way to handle the matter in today's complex business climate. The rule is simple: if you do not understand your cash needs and your cash problems have become a nightmare, ask a professional to assess and explain them to you. If one financial professional cannot help you, find another who can without delay or risk business failure in short order.

2

CASH MANAGEMENT
BY DEFAULT

In the first chapter, I discussed how misunderstanding of cash as a vital part of a successful business operation can not only create problems for owners but also make them indifferent to cash. This lofty attitude of ignoring cash cannot isolate owners from making decisions involving cash. As a result, many of the problems with cash in today's businesses have been further compounded by business owners who make important monetary decisions with a nonchalant attitude toward their effect on the prosperity of their operations. One should bear in mind that, in business, cash is the determining factor at the end of the decision-making process, even though it usually has nothing to do with either the purpose of the business decision or its eventual outcome. Conversely, many very good business decisions can never be contemplated because of lack of funds. Thus, cash is more than just the final arbiter in a business decision: it is the necessary catalyst to the decision-making process.

Cash also serves another need which may seem obvious at first but deserves attention: without sufficient cash funds a business cannot continue to operate. Simple logic, but why do so many businesses collapse from the lack of available cash? Regrettably, many owners are unaware that their actions place a drain on existing cash reserves.

Let's turn our attention to some of the cash practices and policies. Although they are reluctantly implemented and reviewed by most business owners, they affect the monetary activities of most businesses, they continually affect cash reserves, and they dictate the need for an eventual establishment of cash controls over the disbursements of funds.

COMMON CASH PROBLEMS

The following are just a few problems faced by the business owner each day in directing their operations which are not clearly understood by the owner, but nevertheless have a significant impact on cash reserves.

Paying Interest.   Whether you are applying for a loan or have an existing loan on the books, you are already aware that interest rates are tied to the fluctuation in the prime rate, or the rate of interest banks charge their preferred customers. At present, the prime rate has remained fairly constant, but there is no assurance that this situation will continue.

During the late 1970s and early 1980s the interest rates for business owners resembled a roller coaster, rising from 13 to 14 percent to as high as 18 to 20 percent in just a few short months. These extreme fluctuations in interest rates caused many businesses with outstanding loans to fail. And businesses that required capital to purchase inventory often found themselves in a dilemma: many of their anticipated customers never materialized because they could not afford to borrow during times of high interest rates to buy the owner's goods. This left businesses with cash funds allocated to inventory and with high interest rates to pay on outstanding inventory loans.

To complicate the problem further for the small business

owner, the federal administration of that period stepped in with a program to curb inflation by tightening the existing money supply through even higher interest rates. If you were a business owner during those years and survived, no one needs to tell you how important the need for sufficient cash was.

Coping with Inflation.   As business owners you have been experiencing a continual increase in the cost of products and services. Hopefully you have been able to pass these increases on to your customers whenever possible. If, for one reason or another, you have not been able to do this, I am sure that you have felt the effect of the increased cost in reduced profit margins. There is no doubt that inflation has been steadily increasing over the years by percentages on top of earlier increases. The current rate of inflation has leveled off, but most government reports are so broadly based in arriving at an average inflation index that most of the information should be viewed with certain skepticism.

In other words, government statistics reflect changes within large corporations as well as among small businesses, which tends to distort the true picture. A drop in gasoline prices due to a curtailment in production of oil in the Middle East, for example, has a greater effect on the inflation index than on the checkbook balance of the average business owner. Furthermore, if leading economists who concentrate their entire careers on understanding all facets of the economy, including inflation, fail to agree on what our economic status is and what should be done about it, why should you, a small business owner, accept these reports as gospel? It is far better to trust your own instincts and not become complacent regarding inflationary trends reported either by the government or by other agencies. The point to remember is that inflation is still increasing at some rate, the rate itself doesn't matter if it continues to drain your existing working capital.

Maintaining Liquidity.   Business liquidity refers to the availability of cash on hand as well as to the ability to sell short-term investments for immediate funds. Unfortunately, for many business owners, available cash on hand is non-existent, and short-term investments that can be turned into cash are more of a dream than reality. If one considers that every business owner usually starts a business with some cash, why do so many businesses operate on practically no working capital, let alone attempting to establish a position of liquidity? There are many reasons for this state of affairs. One reason is the failure of some business owners to make an initial cash projection before beginning operations. They therefore enter business undercapitalized, having forgotten, or ignored a cardinal rule of business operations.

In my text *The Action-Step Plan to Owning and Operating a Successful Business* the lack of working capital in starting a new business was clearly highlighted by an actual case history.

> Management—the need for proper cash planning—is crucial to the future success of any business. Many business individuals come to me who have already started their own business. I found the majority of these people had no plans whatsoever. As a matter of fact, they were seeking my professional advice because their working capital derived from savings or personal loans was depleted and they had little to show for their entrepreneurial efforts. In many cases what had already been done had to be undone, redirected and even done over in order to gain a hold over a corrective overall business plan. It is sad to realize that one's efforts and money had been placed into the wrong channels and the chances of getting the money back, not to mention payment for their time committed, is highly unlikely. The point at which individuals realize the error of starting a business without advance planning varies. Many people reach the point of no return and simply go under without seeking professional guidance. In this connection I recall a case of a young woman who came to my consulting firm with this problem.
>
> She had started a new business in the competitive record

and tape retail market. In order to have sufficient inventory of tapes and records she had spent three quarters of her initial working capital resources. By the time she came to me her resources were nil. In two months of operation she had depleted most of her capital. Her store was stocked with inventory and she spent what money she had left for initial operating costs. Proper planning of working capital would have enabled her to avoid the obvious by (1) providing enough working capital for the fast moving inventory which requires immediate replacement on popular items and (2) promotional sales programs to move slow moving items from the shelves quickly, thereby replenishing precious working capital and providing money for a sufficient period of time to cover initial expenses and the development of customer following in the marketplace.

In desperation she finally closed her store and sold off what she could. Of course, she never recovered anything close to the amount of her initial investment. She had made the basic and costly mistake too many would-be entrepreneurs make— she had underestimated the need for planning before starting her operation*

Other business owners have failed to plan properly for cash needs by failing to establish a program of cash management. As a consequence, most of these businesses find themselves operating on a shoestring. Survival under this type of operation is discouraging if not impossible; not only must owners try to exist from day to day, but they are unable to make any business moves that might lead to a more profitable operation. In short, they are trapped, victims of their own lack of cash planning, operating in a mode that shuts them out from success.

Providing for the Unexpected. Not even the most conscientious business owner following a program of carefully planned cash management can anticipate every problem that

*Excerpted, with permission, from Emery Toncré, The Action-Step Plan to Owning and Operating a Successful Business (Englewood Cliffs, N.J.: Prentice-Hall, 1983), pp. 19–23.

could require additional funds. Such a situation is often the result of a combination of many other problems coming together at once. For example, how often has the following chain of events happened to you? A sudden drop in bookings is not noticed immediately and leads to a drop in income, which is eventually reversed by placing pressure on the sales and marketing departments. Subsequently, bookings pick up and sales volume is restored to original levels. However, insufficient cash generated from the prior drop in sales causes cash reserves to plunge, and fixed expenses requiring immediate payment drain off what remains of existing working capital while other vendor invoices are held up for future payment.

For some owners the problem can become even more serious. If working capital levels during the drop in bookings are so low that there is not enough left to pay basic fixed costs (incurred at all levels of business activity), you may have to explain to your employees during a period of rising sales, increasing working capital levels, and perhaps even during a need for overtime that you cannot afford to pay them their due wages. Another crisis might occur when production comes to a halt because, for example, funds needed to repair equipment are not available. Nothing has been allocated for this kind of emergency because it was unforeseen. No cash, no production.

Clearly, working capital funds must not only take into consideration operational needs and support the business owner's decisions but also allow for additional cash reserves to cover the unexpected.

Meeting Advanced Payments.   Many business owners are required to invest cash in products or services prior to receiving payment for their efforts. In this case, I am not referring to the simple billing requirements of 60 to 90 days delay before a customer pays you. What I am referring to is the business owner who finds it necessary to invest working capital for completion of services or for the acquisition of products prior to their sale. For example, let's examine the business operaion of a building contractor. A building is constructed on speculation or built to specification. In either case, it requires that the building contractor advance payments from his working funds to various subcontractors, such as electricians, plumbers, heating and cooling contractors, masons and so forth, prior to the completion of the building. Although some builders operate on small working capital budgets and are unable to pay subcontractors on time, most subcontractors expect payment when their portion of the job has been completed. Meeting these demands requires careful financial planning; all work must be completed on time and within the limits of allocated costs, and the costs of supplies to the builder must conform to the estimated expenses allowed in the initial bid price. Builders who fail to follow a carefully planned course of action will subsequently fall victim to the need for additional working funds. This can often lead to business failure if the additional funds are not available.

By the same token, business owners who require advance funds for the purchase of inventory need cash planning. To some extent, their problems can be even more complex than those of a building contractor because they must plan for two additional factors: (1) they must have enough cash to pay for the inventory necessary to stock, and (2) they must choose merchandise that will sell. Consider a business person who operates a lady's boutique. Not only must inventory be bought in advance but the choice of the style of merchandise that will sell must occur four to six months before the merchandise is put on display. It is impossible to carry on this type of activity without planning for working capital needs long in advance. Those who believe it is possible are likely candidates for business failure.

Collecting Cash.   Almost every business owner today is having a problem collecting past due receivables, coping with an ever-increasing number of bad debts, and confronting deliberate delays by customers in their payments against outstanding bills. There was a time when it was considered a binding, moral, and ethical obligation to pay bills on time. Today, the opposite appears to be more acceptable and it is considered a sharp business practice to postpone paying a debt for as long as possible. Today's motto might well be "don't pay anyone until you are paid first." Right or wrong, these changes in practice have created a business atmosphere where as much effort is put into being paid on time as in maintaining good customer relations, product quality, prompt service and speedy delivery of products. As a result, sales personnel today spend as much time collecting receivables as they do marketing their products or services.

Excuses for not paying on time become richly imaginative. How often have you heard "the check is in the mail," "we lost the invoice; please send another," "we only pay our bills during certain times of the month," "we don't believe your invoice is accurate," "we are returning the merchandise for credit," *ad nauseam*.

There is little question why this is so. Insufficient working capital and a tight monetary policy have forced today's business owner to tighten the reins over existing working capital funds. As we have already stated, insufficient working capital is characteristic of most small business owners. However, tight monetary policies by the government to curb inflation have resulted in regulations over the available supply of money, requiring the banker to maintain greater amounts of cash reserves to back outstanding loans. Today's business owners simply do not have enough working capital to cover themselves in a climate of tight monetary policy and maintain their basic business operations at the same time. Consequently, what was yesterday's simple billing and payment procedure has turned into a money-grabbing jungle where the end (avoidance and collection of debt) justifies the means.

Business owners alone have little power to reverse the current trend. As a means of survival, I recommend that you take whatever steps necessary to collect past due invoices. There are a few policies you can initiate to help alleviate the problem, including limiting credit until you know a customer's payment record and never accepting work without making a financial credit check on new customers.

In short, collecting your money for services performed or products sold is no longer a simple procedure. It has become a mean game of survival of the fittest.

Changing Monetary Policies.   Government action affects the small business owner in many ways. The most dramatic effect, if not the most lasting, is the one government action has on the small business owner's available cash reserves. Certain government actions have been the result of IRS actions taken against the business owners. For example, in a recent newsletter the agency announced it has begun to take some steps against the "underground economy" (unreported taxable income). These initial steps have resulted in rather sizable returns.

Since September of 1983 more than $100 million has been collected from taxpayers which include small business owners in the New York Metropolitan area who have failed to report all income as well as wages, interest, dividends, state tax refunds, on their 1981 tax returns. Unreported programs designed to identify taxpayers who fail to declare income from all sources by matching income reported by the taxpayer against income reported by the payer has led to this new policy of follow-up collection activity.

Revenues under the so-called URP Program (Unreported Program) are expected to escalate and bring an additional $100 million annually with the help of newly installed optical character recognition equipment for the information returned processing center. These new systems recognize multifont machine and typewritten characters at the rate of 3,459 form 1099 dot prints per hour. A major form redesign will increase its capacity to 10,800, 1099 forms per hour by February of 1985.

Financial institutions have long been required to report interest and dividends paid to customers and the IRS has always accomplished a 100% review of payer's information recorded on magnetic tape. However, payer's information supplied on paper documents have to be matched by hand. Because the process was so time consuming only about 16% of the forms were matched. Under the new OCR system the efforts will be transferred on paper documents to tapes and allow for 100% review. In addition to new technology, recently enacted regulations require that form 1099 be prepared by all small businesses and reported to the IRS and further close the gap on all unreported income.*

Additional tax burdens are continually being placed on the small business owner by government actions. Over the last 10 years of tax consulting, I have never been able to document one tax decrease that was not somehow offset by a tax increase in another related area. For as long as we have deficit financing as a fiscal policy which allows the government to spend more than it collects in tax revenues, increased taxes seem inevitable.

Government action in the marketplace in the form of defense contracts and economic policies altered to fit foreign policies has also had a profound effect on small business. Such actions by our government has resulted in increased foreign competition from countries such as Taiwan, Korea, and the Dominican Republic, where labor is cheap and products can be produced for less money. For the most part, competition over the long run is healthy for everyone, business and consumers. But abrupt changes in foreign policy that encompass economic sanctions or "perks" can wreak havoc with the small business owners who are not large enough to withstand the sudden shock to their business activity.

Cash planning to ensure your survival is the only defense

*Excerpted from the Internal Revenue Service Director's *Newsletter*, Newark District, June 1984, p. 3.

COMMON CASH PROBLEMS   23

you have against increasing taxes and government economic policies. Use it.

Utilizing Antiquated Accounting Records.   Today's accounting records are detailed and precise in every area. In some cases, they are so laden with supporting schedules that even some professionals find it difficult to determine the current financial status of the business in question. Of course, accuracy is paramount in recordkeeping, but overly complex schedules can often overshadow and obscure the true financial picture. Over the years simplicity in accounting, which resulted in focusing attention on the basic problems causing financial strain, has given way to more detailed and complex records that few business owners have time to read or understand.

Prior to the advent of the computer, it was not uncommon to find business operations inundated with heavy ledgers meticulously kept to the penny. The need for this type of accuracy is questionable. If business owners cannot readily utilize their records to determine their financial cash position on any given day and to project their future needs, the records are useless. Even with the use of today's small business computers, business owners are often hard-pressed to ascertain their exact cash flow positions. Armed with programs made available with the purchase of current computer hardware, many business owners find that these programs perform the functions of balancing the accounts in the records and of aging the accounts receivable or accounts payable, but do little to ascertain the actual cash flow as it relates to current conditions or projected futures. I will have more to say about this matter when I discuss the automation of cash management in Chapter 6, but for now the most important thing to remember is that *updated cash projections are a must* in providing supporting detail to current accounting records.

The business owner's ability to determine his or her current cash position or to project future cash needs is just as important as the ability to accurately record taxable income for tax payments. Accountability for taxes is basic, but sufficient cash flow for survival is mandatory.

Growing Cash Needs from Less Obvious Factors. There are also some lesser-known factors that contribute to cash needs which, if left unattended, could cause a business to fail. Some of these silent cash bleeders are:

1. *Price-Conscious Customers.* Customers today are continually searching for a bargain. If a product meets all their basic requirements, the price of the product or service becomes the determining factor. Pressure to reduce prices place a heavy burden on today's business owners to offset these losses with other actions in order to sustain profits. Thus, to keep profits from shrinking, most business owners place pressure on their suppliers to reduce their prices. In turn, these vendors place pressure on *their* suppliers to reduce prices, and so on until lower prices meet everyone's demands. Of course, getting the best product for the best price is a legitimate goal, but placing price over all other marketing factors eliminates the true purpose of competition and fosters this cycle of bargain hunters. Failure to recognize price-cutting and how it will affect your cash funds could lead to trouble. But if you are able to recognize the effect of price reductions on your cash reserves, you can emphasize the other competitive factors that promote your product and enhance your services, such as quality, service, and promptness.

2. *Changing Breakeven Points.* A breakeven point for a small business is dependent to some degree on a stable base of fixed expenses. Generally, these expenses, which include rent, contract leases, payment of bank loans, certain utilities, and a large portion of payroll, remain at the same level month after month. However, over the last several years business owners have discovered that even so-called fixed expenses

have tended to rise. For example, many rentals based on leases are now subject to increases in the gross national product and are indexed accordingly. Utilities which in the past could be expected to remain within a certain range are subjected to occasional seasonal changes and have been allowed to increase each year by the various state and federal controlling agencies to offset the effects of inflation. Even payroll can no longer be considered constant, given contract changes in wages and increases in the range and costs of fringe benefits. It takes little imagination to understand that when the variable expense areas also increase, a small business without proper expense controls can deplete its profits so quickly that a breakeven point becomes unattainable.

For these reasons, breakeven points can no longer be taken for granted. Today a formerly stable breakeven point can change within three months and a higher breakeven point resulting from reduced profits can make the efforts of a business owner to generate profits an exercise in futility. In short, if he allows costs to become too high, he can never make a profit at *any* level of sales activity. Management pressures to increase sales and reduce expenses may bring about some increased profits over the short term if the business has a reasonable breakeven point. But business owners who fail to monitor their breakeven points from *actual results* cannot determine if their efforts will continue to be profitable over the long term. A single increase in a single fixed expense can create a new problem. Breakeven points are benchmarks for gauging business efforts. Use them wisely.

3. *The High Cost of Opportunities.*   Real business opportunities come along infrequently, and for some business owners the ability to take advantage of a promising opportunity can be as rare as the opportunity itself. The problem is always lack of cash, not lack of motivation. For example, consider the possibility of buying the building you lease at a special price, or buying out your competitor for less money than he or she is worth. Can you honestly say you could take advantage of such opportunities if they arose? Only

those owners with the foresight to plan for this type of "venture" cash will be able to take advantage of opportunities.

As you can see, a business owner encounters various cash needs and must have sufficient cash reserves at all times. There is no way for a business owner to escape making cash decisions, right or wrong, for without cash a business cannot operate, and without a cash management program there *will* be no cash with which to operate. That said, let's move on to fundamentals of a cash management program.

3

THE FUNDAMENTALS OF A CASH MANAGEMENT PROGRAM

The cash management program has one fundamental objective: to sustain sufficient cash reserves (working capital) by controlling all sources of cash income and all disbursements of cash funds. The major thrust of this chapter will be to introduce you to the fundamentals of how the program works, leaving the more detailed action steps of actual implementation to later chapters.

Before we can discuss the factors of the cash management program, you must first understand how the program functions. Let's examine in flow chart sequence how the program works (see Exhibit 3-1). Beginning with a customer analysis, a long-term sales projection is developed for the next 12 to 18 months. From this sales projection fixed expenses (expenses identified by the business owner as remaining constant at all levels of activity) are deducted. In addition to all fixed expenses, variable expenses (expenses that fluctuate with increases and decreases in activity) are also deducted from the sales projection. The net result of these steps represents projected profit for the forecasted period. The ending balance for assets, which include such items as open account

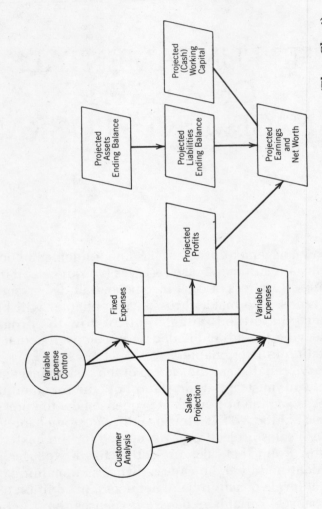

EXHIBIT 3-1. Fundamentals of the Cash Management Program (Flow Chart)

28

receivable, inventory on hand, capital equipment, and corporate investments, is projected at the end of the end of the 12- or 18-month period based on the forecasted activity for that period. The ending balance of all projected liabilities, such as the outstanding accounts payable, corporate debts, and other incurred liabilities is also forecasted at the end of the 12- or 18-month period. The net worth, which consists of capital stock and prior year's earnings, is increased by the projected profits. What remains left to determine is the projected cash (working capital), as shown on Exhibit 3-1.

If we express this equation for further clarification in dollars (see Exhibit 3-2), it would indicate that what we have at this point is merely a profit and loss and balance sheet projection. However, the cash management program has a much broader concept than the simple projection. The program is based on the assumption that all businesses will

EXHIBIT 3-2.   Fundamentals of the Cash Management Program (expressed in dollars)

Projected sales		$ 500,000
Less fixed expenses		100,000
Total		$ 400,000
Less variable expenses		300,000
Total projected profit		$ 100,000
Total assets		$1,000,000
Less total liabilities		700,000
Total		$ 300,000
Less net worth		
Capital stock	$ 50,000	
Prior year's earnings	100,000	
Projected profits	100,000	
Total		$ 250,000
Projected (cash) working capital		$ 50,000

eventually vary from any projection, no matter how well it was prepared. The key question the program must answer is how much the business can be allowed to vary from its projection before all steps to sustain its cash reserves have been exhausted. For example, let's assume that actual sales compared to the projection were $50,000 less than forecasted after three months of operations. If the business was able to compensate for this loss by a reduction in variable expenses until the reason for the sales drop was corrected, the cash reserves would be protected. As you can see, the cash management program has separate control points requiring action by the business owner to stay within the limits of the projection and also to counterbalance the effects of a subpar performance in other areas. Therefore, all elements of the program must be controlled as one unit in order to meet the objective of maintaining sufficient cash reserves to operate the business properly.

Let's now turn our attention to a brief discussion of the essential factors that constitute the framework of the cash management program before proceding to the implementation steps in the next chapter.

BASIC ELEMENTS OF A CASH MANAGEMENT PROGRAM

Long- and Short-Term Cash Projections

One of the essential factors of a cash management program is the establishment of short- and long-term cash projections. For the business owner, a cash projection is the first step toward business planning. Cash projection, an offshoot of business planning, requires that the owner establish goals for plotting his operations along a course designed to result in cash profits. Although far from an exact science, the action of having to project objectives in terms of financial and cash needs compels thought about business decisions in terms of the monetary effect they will have on operations.

The act of projecting cash needs, however, is based upon business operations that are often unpredictable. Therefore, cash projections will have to be altered from time to time. As long as any changes are based upon sound management principles, they should not weaken the projection. Simply changing a cash projection without careful consideration of what effect those changes will have on the conduct of business will defeat the entire purpose of developing a supporting cash projection that meets the objectives of the game plan. To make projections as realistic as possible, owners must develop two projections, long- and short-term.

A long-term projection establishes long-term goals for the business. Because long-term goals are often unobtainable, short-term projections (six months or less) are needed to interface with long-term goals to make the entire exercise more realistic.

Short-term goals reflect a more realistic condition over the nearest six-month period. Changing long-term goals to reflect every change shown by short-term trends is not advisable, but changing long-term goals to reflect continuing *trends* shown in short-term projections is the proper way for the business owner to alter long-term prospects.

Thus, the rule to remember in developing a cash projection is to establish both long- and short-term goals that can be altered only on the basis of sound business decisions. The equation is simple. Business planning requires forecasting cash projection goals. Meeting these goals requires good business judgment and action on the part of business owners. And, finally, achieving these goals will result in cash profits.

Marketing and Sales Projections

The sale of a firm's product or service is usually one of the largest sources of its cash funds. Although commonly understood by most business owners, the actual ability to execute and market one's product effectively is often the most difficult task the business owner must face. Sales don't just materialize out of thin air; a carefully balanced sales program is needed.

One of the essential elements needed to develop an effective sales and marketing program is an ability to convey credibility about the product or service being marketed. Selling succeeds only to the extent that you possess the ability to convince others you have something that they need. If you do not possess a thorough knowledge of your product or service, you will surely fail. In this respect, initial contacts with prospective customers are the most vital since they establish the all-critical first impressions and set the tone for future customer relationships.

Sales promotions are another important tool in any marketing program, as are referrals from satisfied customers and market-sensitive pricing of goods and services. Personalized service is an area of marketing many business owners fail to recognize as a merchandising tool. Advertising, however, is generally recognized as a major marketing factor. Unfortunately, there is no general rule that business owners can follow regarding the amount of funds to set aside for advertising. The problem a business owner must resolve is how to measure the effectiveness of advertising per dollar expended. Finally, effective follow-through with customers on the results of your service or use of your product, along with consideration of diversification of products or services, can widen your merchandise base.

Expense Controls

Variable expense controls are not a new concept; large corporations have been using them for years. But the concept is seldom put to use by small business owners. This oversight can be disastrous where excessive expenses may quickly drain off existing cash reserves. Some owners have been reluctant to accept this particular control concept because they believe that controls over expenses can be helpful to large corporations but impractical for small business. Others think they do not have enough in the way of expenditures to be concerned about controls. Consequently, owners claim it is far too costly to set up a system for controlling expenses and far better to allow them simply to run their course.

In my view, no expense is too small to warrant some type of control. In a large corporation, for example, $30,000 might be the total sum of just one expense item during any given month, but for some small businesses the expenditure of an extra $30,000 could spell the difference between success and failure during the same period. Therefore, the amount of expenditure is not relevant and certainly not the deciding factor in determining the need for a control. If the amount of expense to be placed under control is small, however, the control itself should be simple. Simplicity makes the control easier to understand and less expensive to operate.

Another problem with expense controls in the view of many small business owners is fixing the responsibility for maintaining limits over the amount of expenditures. In many businesses the owner is often the only person who controls disbursements. In such cases, the owner may use one standard over the control of an expense for himself and another for employees. For example, it is far easier for a business owner to put a cap on the traveling expenses of an employee than it is to place such a limit over his or her own expenditures.

Let me describe a case history of one business owner who had such strong feelings about being limited by controls over what he considered to be his own money that he was deadset against any type of control over expenses. My consulting firm was asked to help this owner improve his company's cash flow. It took us only a few days to determine that he was the biggest spender in the company. When we showed him the financial effect his spending spree was having on cash reserves, he finally conceded that he had a right to spend his own money but not to the point of breaking the company.

Balance Sheet and Cash Flow Statements

Most small business owners would be hard-pressed to explain the purpose of the balance sheet in their accounting statements. Moreover, only a handful of business owners can explain the relationship between the balance sheet and cash-on-hand. Understanding just a few simple keys to the more complex details of the balance sheet, however, can make it a revealing cash management tool.

The balance sheet falls into three categories: assets, liabilities and net worth. The relationship between these categories can be defined as *total assets less total liabilities equals net worth.* Some accounting statements restate this equation as total assets equal the sum of total liabilities and net worth.

Assets.   The first category on the balance sheet, assets, includes such items as cash on hand, accounts receivable, and ending inventory. Some assets are already on hand, while others are forthcoming. For example, cash in the bank is usually as available as the nearest bank branch office, while accounts receivable are monies outstanding that are due at some future date and inventory represents the investment of money in stock.

Liquid assets, such as cash in the bank, are assets that are easily acquired. For a small business, especially a business operating with small amounts of working capital, sufficient liquid cash is essential to existence. Businesses that have a high level of cash liquidity are generally called cash-intense. The need for high levels of inventory or sizable accounts receivable tends to make a business less cash-intense and more dependent upon the need for cash controls. The objecive of these controls, as formulated in a cash management program, is the ability to acquire available cash at the proper time. In addition, an effective cash management program will also establish the level of working capital needed to operate a business.

Accounts receivable results from billing your customers for products or services rendered. The rate at which accounts receivable turn over is indicative of how often customers pay. An aging of your accounts receivable is a breakdown of what each customer owes and how long he or she has owed it.

Inventory—and the simple need to maintain it in order to operate a business—places an immediate strain on cash reserves. Business owners who do not have a program that encompasses inventory controls along with controls over cash, accounts receivable, and equipment acquisition as part of their cash management programs, jeopardize their working capital levels and their very existence as viable business operations.

Finally, there are other assets on the average balance sheet of a small business, such as security deposits and the investment of cash reserves, that also affect cash funds but play a lesser role.

Liabilities.   This area of the balance sheet represents expense commitments incurred by the small business owner that are still owed. For example, accounts payable reflects monies due vendors, while outstanding loans are usually due the bank or other individuals who have loaned the business funds.

The most important purpose of the liability side of the balance sheet is to make certain the business does not become overcommitted to debt, placing a future strain on available cash reserves. Once committed to paying a particular disbursement, the liability is then a reality and must sooner or later be paid. Commitment to the liability is a control function of the cash disbursements under an effective cash management program, as is deciding when payment should be made. Both should have a direct correlation to projected sources of available cash income. Remember, a business cannot spend more than it takes in and return a cash profit. And under any effective cash management program, the objective is to return a profit or shareholders' investment.

Net Worth.   The third category of the balance sheet, net worth, consists of capital stock, retained earnings from business operations, and shareholders' investments. These items represent the sum total of what the business is worth. Net worth should not be confused with liquid net worth, which is the total of all cash on hand less the sum of all immediate debts. On the balance sheet, net worth is the final result of the combined efforts of all business actions expressed in terms of dollars and cents which could conceivably be available tomorrow if operations stopped, everything was sold, everyone paid off, and the balance was pocketed.

The most supporting statement to the balance sheet is the cash flow statement, which details the changes that have occurred in the balance sheet from one period to another. The ability of a business owner to understand the profit and loss statement as it relates to the balance sheet and the balance sheet as it relates to the cash flow statement will provide any owner with just about every essential financial tool available to effectively operate a cash management project.

The significant relationship among these various financial statements is explained in the following quotation and exhibit, taken from *How To Read A Financial Report*, by John A. Tracy.

A company's cash flow statement begins with an analysis of the cash flow effect from . . . those transactions involved in making sales and incurring expenses . . .

Cash flow analysis of operations starts with the amount of net income from the income statement. However, changes in the operating assets and operating liabilities during the year usually cause cash flow from operations to be quite different from net income for the year, which is currently true in this case. Please note Exhibit [3.3] and the lines extending from the operating assets and operating liabilities into the cash flow statement. *Negative cash flow factors are those changes*

EXHIBIT 3-3. Balance Sheet Cash Flow Illustration ($ per /000)

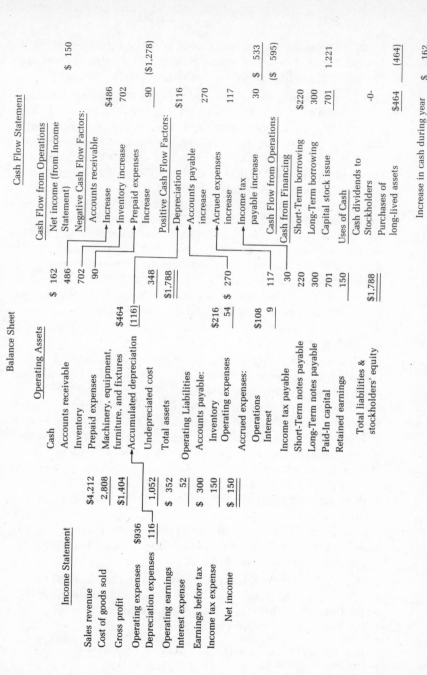

Income Statement

Sales revenue		$4,212
Cost of goods sold		2,808
Gross profit		$1,404
Operating expenses	$936	
Depreciation expenses	116	1,052
Operating earnings		$ 352
Interest expense		52
Earnings before tax		$ 300
Income tax expense		150
Net income		$ 150

Balance Sheet

Operating Assets

Cash		$ 162
Accounts receivable		486
Inventory		702
Prepaid expenses		90
Machinery, equipment, furniture, and fixtures	$464	
Accumulated depreciation	(116)	
Undepreciated cost		348
Total assets		$1,788

Operating Liabilities

Accounts payable:		
Inventory	$216	
Operating expenses	54	$ 270
Accrued expenses:		
Operations	$108	
Interest	9	117
Income tax payable		30
Short-Term notes payable		220
Long-Term notes payable		300
Paid-In capital		701
Retained earnings		150
Total liabilities & stockholders' equity		$1,788

Cash Flow Statement

Cash Flow from Operations

Net income (from Income Statement)		$ 150
Negative Cash Flow Factors:		
Accounts receivable Increase	$486	
Inventory increase	702	
Prepaid expenses Increase	90	($1,278)
Positive Cash Flow Factors:		
Depreciation	$116	
Accounts payable increase	270	
Accrued expenses increase	117	
Income tax payable increase	30	$ 533
Cash Flow from Operations		($ 595)

Cash from Financing

Short-Term borrowing	$220	
Long-Term borrowing	300	
Capital stock issue	701	1,221
Uses of Cash		
Cash dividends to Stockholders	-0-	
Purchases of long-lived assets	$464	(464)
Increase in cash during year		$ 162

37

in operating assets and liabilities that decrease the cash flow from operations (net income). Positive cash flow factors are those changes that increase cash flow. [Italics added.]

Accounts receivable increased $486,000 during the year which means that $486,000 of its sales revenue for the year had not been received in cash by the end of the year. Only $3,726,000 of company's sales revenue was actually collected in cash. ($4,212,000 sales revenue less $486,000 accounts receivable equals $3,726,000 in cash received.) So the $486,000 increase in accounts receivable during the year is a negative cash flow factor that decreases the amount of available cash funds on hand. Next, inventory on hand was $702,000 at the end of the year. The $702,000 represents potential cash funds which still have to be collected. Prepaid expenses were $90,000 during the year. In addition, to its regular operating expenses, the company had to prepay $90,000 for next year's expenses. This $90,000 places another demand on the available cash reserves. Up to this point things look pretty bad. The three cash flow factors add up to a $1,278,000 restriction on cash reserves.

However, on the other side of the coin as it were, the company did not have to pay out in cash the entire amount of expenses reported on the income statement. These unpaid expenses are the positive cash flow factors which add funds to the cash flow statement. First of all, depreciation expense is not a cash outlay. When the depreciation expense increased the accumulated depreciation amount which was deducted from the asset account, the asset account, not cash, was decreased. So depreciation expense is a positive cash flow factor. . . . [T]hree liabilities are directly affected by the expenses of the business—accounts payable, accrued expenses, and income tax payable. An increase in any operating liability during the year means that cash was not disbursed and the working capital reserve was not depleted.

To sum up: starting with $150,000 net income deducting the $1,278,000 negative cash flow factors and adding the $533,000 positive cash flow factors gives the negative $595,000 cash flow from operations.*

*Excerpted, with permission, from John A. Tracy, *How to Read a Financial Report* (New York: Wiley, 1983), pp. 70–71.

Employee Relations

Let me begin this section by citing an actual case history of a client who found himself with an employee relations problem far more serious than the simple action of hiring or firing workers.

This client owned a machine shop operation that consisted of five employees, two of whom were capable of operating all the machinery in the plant. Machinists with this type of experience are classified as tool and die makers and are difficult to find because very few people have acquired their skills. Those who have are in constant demand and usually find work easily. The owner in this case, well aware of the job market, felt that there was little he could do about the demand in the labor market for these workers and, as a consequence, allowed both men to keep erratic work schedules, to demand and receive increased wages on request, and to participate in the large bonuses usually set aside for management at year end. The question in this case revolved around what the owner could have done to prevent the virtual blackmail exerted by these two highly skilled employees.

Had the owner initiated a program designed to provide backup employees by training apprentices, the problem would never have arisen. Management could have immediately moved a few partially trained apprentices into these crucial jobs and with a certain degree of extra supervision regained control over their operations. As it turned out, one of the two tool and die makers left the company and the other remained—as an unwanted partner.

Establishing work standards for employees is a vital facet of any cash management program. This is a new concept for most small business owners, who generally consider work standards unnecessary and too costly for their operations. On the contrary, considerable profit can be lost to inefficient employees, and work standards for employees in a small business operation can be effective in increasing productivity and profits.

For example, employee turnover is a serious problem for most small business owners. How does a small owner cope with this? Although it can be difficult, careful hiring practices, more time spent investigating employee attitudes and desires, and the payment of incentives to productive employees will often make the difference.

Special attention, flexibility, and close working relationships with employees can be a definite advantage for the small business owner, an advantage that many larger companies do not enjoy. In a small business, employees can feel more like part of a family, especially if the owner uses first names on the job and shows more of a personal interest in individual problems. Successful cash management programs require a steady workforce, and happy employees with few morale problems ensure better productivity and lower labor turnover.

Cash Investment

Investing surplus cash in commercial areas (such as bank CDs, commercial paper bonds, and other government investments) is another basic of a comprehensive cash management program. The object is to make money on money. Large business operations, with the help of their treasurers, have been investing surplus funds for years. Small business operations have not given this area much attention, however, probably because 90 percent of new business owners start operations on a shoestring, spending all of their cash until it is depleted. The remaining 10 percent survive on what they consider to be better business judgment, even though they still suffer from a lack of sufficient working capital. Thus, the last thing most business owners consider is what to do with surplus cash.

Yet there exists in every business a time during its lifespan when surplus cash actually becomes available. This generally occurs sometime after the initial growth period. Most business owners fail to recognize this particular time in their business operations and thus fail to take the opportunity to reinvest surplus cash for additional profits. Other business owners are simply afraid to reinvest surplus funds after years of suffering without sufficient working capital. There is no excuse for this type of inaction.

On the other hand, some business owners feel surplus cash is a signal to initiate various "get-rich-quick schemes." After years of growth, when cash was tight and the owner found it difficult to stay afloat, the temptation is great to jump into all types of plans that promise almost everything and usually result in nothing. Such ill-considered actions often lead owners into eventual business failure. The sad commentary is that cash that could have been placed in a liquid investment to generate a quick return is often thrown into schemes that result in failure.

An effective cash management program recognizes that the proper use of surplus cash is to place funds into commercial investments where the money is safe and easily obtainable. Longer term investments such as the acquisition of the building where the business owner operates may prove very profitable over a longer period, but requires more careful planning and extensive cash projections on the part of the business owner.

Utilizing Professionals

As a business owner you will soon come to realize that the professionals are the only objective partners you may currently have in business. They can afford to be objective with their advice because they have no personal responsibility for the operation of your business. Of course, they would like to see you succeed, but many professionals have learned over the years that although many small business operators usually listen to their advice, they do not always follow it. As a business owner, you must make the final decision regarding the acceptance of any advice from a professional. The most serious problem I have encountered as a small business consultant is that many business owners do not understand what a professional is supposed to do for them. Therefore, as a precautionary measure they reject all advice, good or bad. Some business owners actually become highly protective of their business after receiving help from a professional. They feel that the professional is in some way overstepping his or her authority and actually running their businesses for them. Unfortunately, in some cases, they are right.

All of this confusion between you as a business owner and the professional adds nothing to your operations. Nevertheless, the need for survival in your business and the fundamental implementation of the cash management program is totally dependent upon the constructive input of qualified professionals. Professional small business consultants are considered to be the best qualified to advise the businessperson on a proper course of action. As generalists who must possess a basic understanding of all the professional business disciplines and skills, they can also help identify the right professional specialist for you to consult to solve a particular problem, whether it be an accountant, a banker, an attorney, a marketing advisor, or a tax advisor.

Therefore, professional accountants are specialists in the field of records, financial matters, and tax problems. As professionals, they make an accountability of how well you have done financially with your operations. Bankers serve several functions necessary to the successful operation of your cash management program. They can provide you with a line of credit that will afford you a greater degree of flexibility with your working capital, provide you with interest on surplus cash investments, loan you money to buy inventory in advance of sales, in some cases factor your accounts receivable, and finally, offer you financial advice.

There are also many other professionals, such as attorneys, investment advisors, employee search consultants, insurance agents, tax advisors, and so forth, who play a role in the execution of your cash management program from time to time. The professionals you will most likely use to execute a proper cash management program, however, will be the small business consultant, accountant, and banker. Using them effectively will enhance your chances of success.

4

IMPLEMENTATION

In this chapter, the implementation steps necessary to establish a cash management program will be shown for a former client, whom we will call the ABC Company. It will begin with the development of the initial cash projection and the other action steps required to modify the initial cash projection in order to protect and sustain a reasonable level of working capital. You will learn how the combined management tools of planning, control, and action steps can alter cash flow and existing levels of working capital. You will see how a business can become cash poor from inaction and failure to utilize its cash management program and ultimately how ABC Company planned, stumbled, and regained the initiative with a cash management program.

ACTION STEP 1: PROJECTING SALES

The first cash management step for the ABC Company was to develop a cash projection of its annual sales (see Exhibit 4-1, which is a summary of the results of actions taken by this company with its customers. In order to develop a base for projecting sales, a review of former sales activity was conducted for each of ABC's customers. Each customer's marketing relationship and previous sales were carefully

EXHIBIT 4-1. ABC Company Sales Projection Compared to First Quarter Actual

	First Year Annual Sales	Second Year Annual Sales	Third Year Annual Sales	Projected Annual Sales	First Quarter Initial Projected Sales	First Quarter Actual Sales
Jones Company	$ 300,000	$ 300,000	$ 400,000	$ 530,000	$132,500	$125,000
Smith Company	200,000	250,000	-0-	-0-	-0-	-0-
Able Inc.	400,000	500,000	600,000	500,000	125,000	120,000
Data Company	100,000	100,000	100,000	100,000	25,000	-0-
Any Company	150,000	120,000	90,000	90,000	22,500	-0-
XYZ Company	550,000	600,000	-0-	-0-	-0-	-0-
Total	$1,700,000					
James Company		50,000	70,000	125,000	31,250	30,000
J&B Inc.		20,000	50,000	75,000	18,750	20,000
Total		$1,940,000				
Annual Growth Percentage		114%				
Book Inc.			100,000	100,000	25,000	15,000
CBT Company			200,000	-0-	-0-	-0-
First Quarter Misc. Increase for Contingencies					10,000	
Total			$1,490,000			
Annual Growth Percentage			77%			
Total				$1,520,000	$390,000	$310,000

studied over the previous three years. The purpose of this customer review was to identify and determine what products each customer had purchased, what physical changes have been made to each customer's product, how customer needs and buying practices had changed and what ABC Company could expect in future sales, given its present customer base. The review consisted of an in-depth study of the buying practices of each customer, designed to reveal seasonal demands, customer problems with respect to lead time between an order and delivery, and the average size of prior orders placed by the customer.

Let's examine the review made by ABC with respect to each customer.

1. *Jones Company.* Over the past several years the relationship with this company has been stable. The product they buy is one ABC Company will continue to produce as long as the Jones Company utilizes the same component parts in the manufacturing of their products. The product has not been seasonal and therefore caused no problem whatsoever to the ABC's present production schedule. The relationship between the two companies has never been better and at this point the ABC Company considered the Jones Company to be one of the best customers. With all of these pluses, sales were forecasted for next year to increase.

2. *Smith Company.* During the first two years of the marketing effort with the Smith Company, the overall relationship was excellent, showing promise of continued growth. During the third year, the Smith Company requested a redesign and a new price quotation on all component parts under production. The ABC Company responded with design changes even though they were directed towards reducing the cost of the product. The Smith Company reviewed the changes and gave the ABC Company its tentative stamp of approval. Three weeks passed without any further word from the customer. During this time, no action was taken by ABC Company to contact Smith. In fact, ABC Com-

pany considered the approval to be more or less academic, but during the fourth week, the ABC sales manager made a routine call on the Smith Company and discovered to his surprise that Smith Company had placed the order for the redesigned product with one of ABC's competitors.

The consequences of this sizable loss of business from the Smith Company resulted in a reorganization of the marketing department within ABC Company. A directive was issued stating that complacency in communications with existing customers would no longer be tolerated. From a projection standpoint, the damage had already been done and it was decided that no further effort would be put forth to recapture the loss.

3. *Able Inc.*   Like the Jones Company, Able Inc. had been a steady customer for years. Communications between the two companies had always been excellent. No problems were anticipated. Expected delivery, production lead time, and timely payment to ABC Company were all considered pluses. Therefore, Able Inc. was projected at $500,000, the average over the last three years.

4. *Data Company.*   Over the years, Data experienced continual problems with the ABC Company, even though their relationship began when both companies were just starting up. Data Company never pursued an aggressive marketing program, starting with only three major companies and continuing to base its entire operation around these three customers. On the other hand, ABC Company always pushed for a marketing program based on diversification and expansion. Working with Data Company to supply products where the marketing program was based on three customers was perceived as risky by ABC. But the real problem that concerned ABC Company was how to effectively forecast future sales with a company whose entire marketing program was questionable. In view of these circumstances it was decided to project Data Company at its previous sales level without any anticipation of growth.

5. *Any Company.* Any Company experienced internal problems which reduced its overall growth over the last several years. Since none of these problems has anything to do with the present customer relationship with ABC Company, a downward trend was projected to continue with ABC projecting the same level as the year before.

6. *The XYZ Company.* The XYZ Company operated an aggressive and thorough marketing program. Component parts manufactured by ABC had to meet rigid standards and delivery time was critical. On top of these requirements, the price paid for the component was always scrutinized. Because of their aggressive marketing program, the XYZ Company was known to constantly change suppliers. The relationship over the past few years had been good for ABC, but XYZ Company, as expected, was eventually lost to a competitor. The likelihood of regaining the XYZ Company business was slim, and therefore no further bookings were projected.

7. *Other Customers.* The remaining four companies, James Company, J&B Inc., Book Inc., and CBT Company had been customers for ABC Company for less than two years. Although their volume was small, they all showed promise of future growth except CBT Company, which ABC Company lost to competition.

As you can see, the development of a sales projection requires careful review of each customer. This process can be further complicated by the fact that customer relationships are constantly changing and therefore require continual review and assessment. As you can see from Exhibit 4-1, the net result of this in-depth customer review is an annual sales projection of $1,520,000 (approximately $127,000 per month). Note that ABC's first quarter projection was $390,000, broken down monthly to $130,000. Actual sales for ABC Company during the first quarter was a total of $310,000. This represents a drop in sales volume from the first quarter projected sales volume of $80,000 ($390,000 projected sales less $310,000 of actual sales).

When the ABC Company analyzed the $80,000 difference customer by customer, the reasons for the drop became apparent (see Exhibit 4-1). For example, during the first quarter the Jones Company showed a sales volume of $125,000 compared to a projected sales volume of $132,500. The $7500 drop in actual sales, however, was not considered serious enough to warrant any adjustment to the sales projection.

Able Inc. also showed a slight drop in the first quarter actual sales from the initial projection of $125,000. As in the case of the Jones Company, the sales drop of $5000 from the projected sales of $125,000 to an actual first quarter of $120,000 was not considered serious enough to warrant an adjustment to the sales projection.

James Company and J&B Inc. were close to target, although Book Inc. was off by $10,000 in the first quarter results compared to projected results. ABC contacted Book Inc. and was informed that the anticipated volume for the first quarter would carry over to the second quarter of the year, placing them on target at the end of June.

The information received from the Data Company and Any Company was not very encouraging. Data Company had lost one of its three customers. Although ABC Company had always harbored this concern, the reality of losing Data's sales still came as a surprise, and no contingency plans by ABC had ever been established to cover the possibility of the loss of business. As a result, there was little left to do but wait for further developments.

Any Company was still experiencing internal problems. Although Any Company was projected to continue in a downward trend with some sales activity, the actual results in the first quarter were zero compared to a projected $22,500. In short, a drop in sales to zero by the Any Company was anticipated. However, ABC still hoped eventually to sell its initial projected annual sales of $90,000 in component parts before year end. Therefore, the Any Company's sales forecast was left unchanged.

As a result of the poor first quarter sales results, the ABC Company was now faced with the problem of the effect they would have on its projected expense control. As you will see later in this chapter, the profit and loss expense control is flexible and should drop in correlation to a decrease in sales. Therefore, the question remaining is whether the actual expenses dropped to the proper projected expense levels or increased over projection, causing another additional strain on cash profits.

ACTION STEP 2: PROFIT AND LOSS
EXPENSE CONTROL

Profit and loss expenses are deductible from sales income. Unlike other cash disbursements, which have a direct effect only on available cash, profit and loss expenditures can decrease both available cash funds *as well as* business profits subject to federal and state corporate taxes. Profit and loss expenditures can be classified into three categories when correlated against sales activity: fixed expenses, semivariable expenses, and directly variable expenses. Fixed expenses, when correlated with sales activity, remain constant at all levels of sales volume (see Exhibit 4-2). Semivariable expenses represent expenses that have both fixed and variable elements in them. And variable expenses are those that are directly related to sales activity.

ABC Company's expenses for each category (fixed, semivariable, and variable) were projected at various levels of sales. To accomplish this, each profit and loss expense was first classified into one of the three categories. The previous year's level of each of the various expenses was plotted onto separate expense graphs to establish a correlation to sales activity (glance at Exhibits 4-5 through 4-23). The plotting

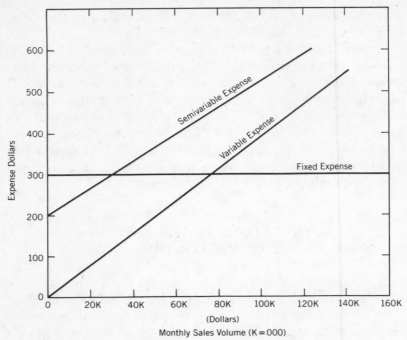

EXHIBIT 4-2.   Expense Chart

of expenses related to sales activities not only established a historical trend line for each expense but reaffirmed its initial classification as a fixed, semivariable, or variable expense. Note that in plotting expenses to sales activity, some expenses failed to conform to any expense pattern when correlated to sales. When this happened, the expenses in question were reviewed by ABC Company to determine why they failed to correlate with a given sales activity and thus did not fall within a general correlation pattern (see Exhibit 4-7). In 90 percent of the cases reviewed, ABC found that the expense items in question were often one-time expenditures unlikely to reoccur. In order to establish a valid projected trend line and correct historical trend, it was necessary to disregard these types of nonrecurring expenses. Once the historical trend line was established for each expense, the next task was to establish a projected expense trend line for each expense.

Since the projection of expense at various levels of sales was designed to be used in conjunction with ABC's cash management program, the projected expense trend lines (as shown on each of ABC's expense charts, Exhibits 4-5 through 4-23) were not arbitrarily established at a flat 10 percent below the historical trend line but only after careful assessment which I will discuss later in this chapter.

Next, it was necessary to identify what individual within ABC would be in a position to control commitments of various expenditures. For example, in establishing control over purchasing (Exhibit 4-19), it was determined that several people could commit ABC Company to buying resale material. To make the matter even more confusing, each individual within the group usually had no knowledge of what was being committed by his or her colleagues. Thus, to ensure control over such expenditures, ABC appointed one individual to keep a running tally on all commitments to ensure that total expenditures did not exceed the total projection at any given level of sales activity. Thereafter, individuals within the group found it beneficial to meet and plan their expense commitments together. This type of profit and loss control over expenses carried the area of responsibility for meeting ABC's projections down to the most basic level of commitment, the individuals and coworkers who actually commit ABC to an expense.

As time progressed and the system became better understood within the company, upper management was able to call on these lowest levels of management to supply expense projections, thereby building a profit and loss projection from the bottom up. At this point, the system was no longer a one-way street on which the worker was expected to restrain his or her expense commitments within projected sales levels directed from top management. Now it had become a team objective, requiring joint effort and the mutual understanding of all those responsible for maintaining a specific expense level in accordance with the company's projection.

Let's now turn our attention to the results of the first quarter for the ABC Company by first reviewing the figures on Exhibit 4-3. This exhibit shows the comparison between the initial projections and the actual results for January, February, and March for sales and expenses. For example, in January the initial projection for sales was $130,000, compared to the actual results of $120,000. The February comparison was $130,000 projected sales compared to $100,000 of actual, and in March $130,000 projected sales compared to $90,000. Total expenses for January, February, and March were projected at $60,700 for each month; the actual expenses in January were $55,450, February $61,500, and March $52,100. The end result of the sales and expense activity showed a projected profit of $7,300 for each of the three months compared to an actual $14,500 profit in January, $500 profit in February, and $28,100 loss in March. What can we learn about the first quarter results of ABC Company from this exhibit? Frankly, very little, unless we analyze the results further.

It is true that Exhibit 4-3 does reflect the drop in sales volume from the initial projections. What it fails to reflect is the adjustment of projected expense control to the actual sales volume. For example, in the month of January expenses were adjusted in total to $57,635 to reflect the drop in volume from $130,000 to $120,000 (see Exhibit 4-4). The $57,635 adjusted expense level in January is the combined expense total determined from reading each expense chart (Exhibits 4-5 through 4-23) at January's sales volume of $120,000. If we examine Exhibit 4-5, the adjusted expense target for $120,000 of sales volume in January was $3,750. If we examine Exhibit 4-7, the adjusted expense target for $120,000 of sales volume in January was $2,500. The same approach can be made with all of the Expense Charts for each month.

What rules can we draw from these exhibits? (1) If ABC Company at the point shown in Exhibit 4-3 had gone no further, the analysis of the results from this exhibit would have been inconclusive, and (2) a business cannot compare its initial projected expenses to actual expenses and draw any valid conclusion; it simply defeats the purpose of the flexible expense control.

Given the aforementioned two rules, what were the actual results for ABC in the first quarter? In January, ABC lost sales of $10,000 from its initial projection. On the other hand, returned sales were $2,000 less than projection, and expenses in total compared to adjusted expenses were $2,185 under projection. As a consequence, the net profit of $14,550 compared to an adjusted projection of $10,365 provided a favorable variance in profit of $4,185. (See Exhibits 4-3 and 4-4.) In February, ABC lost $30,000 in sales from its initial projection. Sales returns were $4,000 less than projection but expenses exceeded the projection by $10,830. In March, sales dropped by $40,000 from the initial projection. Although sales returns were favorable by $6,000, expenses exceeded the projection by $4,045 (see Exhibits 4-3 and 4-4). We have already reviewed the cause for the sales drop, so let's turn our attention to a careful examination of what happened to ABC's expense control during the first quarter.

General Taxes and Payroll Taxes

Taxes are a semivariable expense item closely allied to ABC's profits and the gross payroll. This expense is considered to be semivariable because of the need for withholding taxes for employees; these taxes are required to be on hand even if sales activity drops to zero. Although we have correlated the tax liability to the level of sales activity, ABC first had to generate profits to incur federal and state taxes and pay employees in order to be subject to payroll taxes such as withholding and social security. In the case of the ABC

EXHIBIT 4-3. ABC Company Profit and Loss, First Quarter (initial projected sales and expense compared to actual)

	January		February		March	
	Initial Projection	Actual	Initial Projection	Actual	Initial Projection	Actual
Sales	$130,000	$120,000	$130,000	$100,000	$130,000	$90,000
Earned Interest	5,000	5,000	5,000	5,000	5,000	5,000
Total Income	$135,000	$125,000	$135,000	$105,000	$135,000	$95,000
Less Returns	12,000	10,000	12,000	8,000	12,000	6,000
Net Income	$123,000	$115,000	$123,000	$97,000	$123,000	$89,000
"Less Cost of Sales	50,000	40,000	50,000	30,000	50,000	60,000
Gross Profit	$73,000	$75,000	$73,000	$67,000	$73,000	$29,000
Less Expenses						
General/Payroll Taxes	3,900	3,900	3,900	3,900	3,900	2,900
Rent	5,000	5,000	5,000	5,000	5,000	5,000
Repair and Maintenance	2,500	2,000	2,500	2,000	2,500	2,000
Gross Payroll	20,000	20,000	20,000	20,000	20,000	20,000
Insurance	1,200	1,000	1,200	1,000	1,200	800
Professional Fee	500	500	500	500	500	500
Interest Expense	2,500	2,500	2,500	2,500	2,500	2,500

Advertising	800	800	800	1,500	800	1,200
Auto-Truck	1,800	1,500	1,800	1,300	1,800	1,000
Dues-Subscriptions	300	200	300	200	300	300
Office Supplies	900	500	900	700	900	800
Telephone	1,200	1,000	1,200	1,300	1,200	1,000
Utilities	750	700	750	850	750	600
Operating Supplies	8,500	6,000	8,500	9,000	8,500	7,000
Travel	6,000	5,000	6,000	7,000	6,000	3,000
Uniforms	350	350	350	250	350	–0–
Entertainment	3,000	3,000	3,000	4,000	3,000	2,000
Contract Service	1,500	1,500	1,500	500	1,500	1,500
Total Expenses	$ 60,700	$ 55,450	$ 60,700	$ 61,500	$ 60,700	$ 52,100
Operating Profit	12,300	19,550	12,300	5,500	12,300	(23,100)
Less Depreciation	5,000	5,000	5,000	5,000	5,000	5,000
Net Profit	$ 7,300	$ 14,500	$ 7,300	$ 500	$ 7,300	$ (28,100)
ᵃCost of Sales						
Opening Inventory	$ 20,000	$ 20,000	$ 20,000	$ 70,000	$ 20,800	$110,000
Purchase Resale Material	80,000	90,000	80,000	70,000	80,000	50,000
Total	100,000	110,000	100,000	140,000	100,000	160,000
Less Ending Inventory	50,000	70,000	50,000	110,000	50,000	100,000
Cost of Sales	50,000	40,000	50,000	30,000	50,000	60,000

EXHIBIT 4-4. ABC Company Profit and Loss, First Quarter

	January		
	Adjusted Sales & Exp.	Actual	Variance
Sales	$120,000	$120,000	$ –0–
Earned Interest	5,000	5,000	–0–
Total Income	$125,000	$125,000	$ –0–
Less Returns	12,000	10,000	2,000
Net Income	113,000	115,000	2,000
Less Cost of Sales	40,000	40,000	–0–
Gross Profit	$ 73,000	$ 75,000	$ 2,000
Less Expenses			
General/Payroll Taxes	3,750	3,900	(150)
Rent	5,000	5,000	–0–
Repair & Maintenance	2,500	2,000	500
Gross Payroll	19,000	20,000	(1,000)
Insurance	1,100	1,000	100
Professional Fee	450	500	(50)
Interest Expense	2,500	2,500	–0–
Advertising	750	800	(50)
Auto/Truck	1,700	1,500	200
Dues/Subscriptions	260	200	60
Office Supplies	850	500	350
Telephone	1,100	1,000	100
Utilities	700	700	–0–
Operating Supplies	8,000	6,000	2,000
Travel	5,500	5,000	500
Uniforms	325	350	(25)
Entertainment	2,750	3,000	(250)
Contract Services	1,400	1,500	(100)
Total Expenses	$ 57,635	$ 55,450	$ 2,185
Operating Profit	15,365	19,550	4,185
Less Depreciation	5,000	5,000	–0–
Net Profit	$ 10,365	$ 14,550	$ 4,185
*Cost of Sales			
Opening Inventory	$ 45,000	$ 20,000	$ 25,000
Purchase Resale Material	75,000	90,000	(15,000)
Total	120,000	110,000	10,000
Less Ending Inventory	80,000	70,000	10,000
Cost of Sales	$ 40,000	$ 40,000	$ –0–

adjusted sales volume and expense control compared to actual)

	February			March		
Adjusted Sales & Exp.	Actual	Variance	Adjusted Sales & Exp.	Actual	Variance
$100,000	$100,000	$ –0–	$ 90,000	$ 90,000	$ –0–
5,000	5,000	–0–	5,000	–0–	–0–
$105,000	$105,000	$ –0–	$ 95,000	$ 95,000	$ –0–
12,000	8,000	4,000	12,000	6,000	6,000
93,000	97,000	4,000	83,000	89,000	6,000
40,000	30,000	10,000	50,000	60,000	(10,000)
$ 53,000	$ 67,000	$ 14,000	$ 33,000	$ 29,000	$ (4,000)
3,250	3,900	(650)	3,000	2,900	100
5,000	5,000	–0–	5,000	5,000	–0–
2,000	2,000	–0–	1,750	2,000	(250)
17,500	20,000	(2,500)	17,000	20,000	(3,000)
1,000	1,000	–0–	900	800	100
400	500	(100)	350	500	(150)
2,450	2,500	(50)	2,500	2,500	–0–
600	1,500	(900)	550	1,200	(650)
1,400	1,300	100	1,270	1,000	270
220	200	20	210	300	(90)
700	700	–0–	625	800	(175)
950	1,300	(350)	850	1,000	(150)
625	850	(225)	600	600	–0–
6,500	9,000	(2,500)	6,000	7,000	(1,000)
4,500	7,000	(2,500)	4,125	3,000	1,125
275	250	25	250	–0–	250
2,250	4,000	(1,750)	2,050	2,000	50
1,050	500	550	1,025	1,500	(475)
$ 50,670	$ 61,500	$(10,830)	$ 48,055	$ 52,100	$ (4,045)
2,330	5,550	(3,170)	(15,055)	(23,100)	(8,045)
5,000	5,000	–0–	5,000	5,000	–0–
$ (2,670)	$ 500	$ (2,170)	$ (20,055)	$(28,100)	$ (8,045)
$ 80,000	$ 70,000	$ 10,000	$100,000	$110,000	$ 10,000
60,000	70,000	(10,000)	50,000	50,000	–0–
140,000	140,000	–0–	150,000	160,000	10,000
100,000	110,000	10,000	100,000	100,000	–0–
$ 40,000	$ 30,000	$ 10,000	$ 50,000	$ 60,000	$ 10,000

Company, there were months when no profits were generated, but there was never a month without payroll and its related taxes.

The historical plotting (Exhibit 4-5) shows a fairly consistent pattern, with the exception of one or two months' activity where an estimated tax payment was made to cover anticipated profits.

Projecting a tighter expense control (i.e., a lower projected trend line on the graph), which anticipates less taxes in face of greater sales activity, seems contradictory. But in the case of the ABC Company, federal tax payments were expected to be smaller because of the adoption of a major pension program, which would divert some cash profits from general taxes into a retirement plan. Furthermore, payroll-related taxes were expected to drop, in spite of higher levels of sales activity, because of increasing employee productivity.

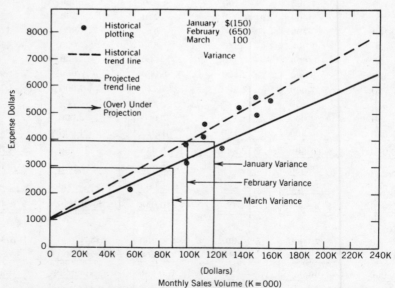

EXHIBIT 4-5.   ABC Company General Taxes and Payroll Taxes Expense Chart

The results from the first quarter show that January and February were overprojected by $150 and $650 respectively; March was underprojected by $100. Thus, no action was considered necessary by ABC to adjust the current expense projection for this time.

Rent

Rent is considered a fixed expense. It remains constant at all levels of sales activity as long as the ABC Company continues to lease its present premises under the same terms (Exhibit 4-6). Since no actual change in the amount paid for rent occurred in the first quarter and no anticipated change was contemplated in the near future, no adjustment was made in the projection.

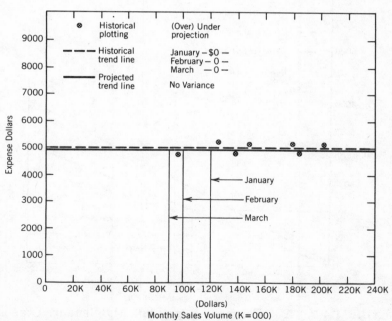

EXHIBIT 4-6.   ABC Company Rent Expense Chart

Repairs and Maintenance

This expense is a combination of two factors: repairs to component parts in accordance with established quality standards and general maintenance of existing facilities.

In plotting the history of this expense (Exhibit 4-7), ABC Company found the general maintenance expenditure to be fairly consistent with sales activity, but the expenditure for repairs to component parts varied more widely when correlated to sales activity because the complexity of the work often caused the expense to increase irrespective of sales volume. The biggest change in expenses occurred when items were returned to ABC in large lots. With this mixed expense history, repairs for components were therefore averaged between the highest and the lowest expenses.

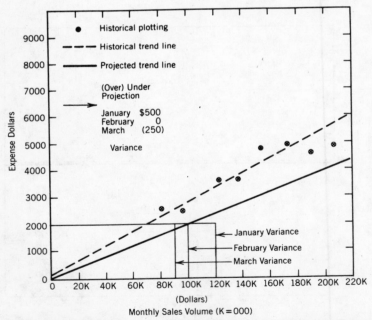

EXHIBIT 4-7.   ABC Company Repair and Maintenance Expense Chart

The projected trend line was intentionally lowered on the graph from historical plottings on the premise that changes in the repair department could be made to reduce the problem of uneven repair-flow resulting from random returns. To accomplish this, repair parts were rerouted and preclassified by the severity and the nature of the problem in order that the item could be sent directly to the proper work station. These changes in repair operation succeeded, as first quarter results showed: January results were underprojected by $500, February was at breakeven, and March was only overprojected by $250.

Gross Payroll

This expense control represents the total payroll, including hourly employees, salaried workers, and officers. Gross payroll is a semivariable expense because employees will be needed even if the activity drops to zero.

The historical pattern of ABC's gross payroll reflected a flatter slope in the historical trendline, typical of a semivariable expense (Exhibit 4-8). As previously mentioned, the ABC Company expected to increase sales activity without increasing the number of workers by stepping up the level of productivity. In addition, production flow was redirected to shorten the existing cycle, and incentive standards were adopted to reward workers for additional efforts.

January was over the initial projection by $1000, February by $2500, and March by $3000. With these results, the ABC Company began to wonder if the productivity program was working. It was my contention that a productivity program of this magnitude would take more than a few months to become fully effective. I therefore suggested to ABC that no changes by made in the initial projection until the results of the productivity program were fully developed and could properly be evaluated over an extended time period.

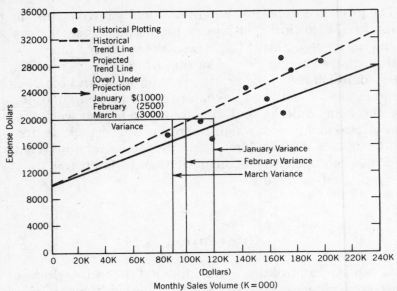

EXHIBIT 4-8.   ABC Company Gross Payroll Expense Chart

Insurance

Insurance expense is a combination of several types of insurance plans: liability, theft, fire security, product, workers' compensation, and medical plans. Because insurance needs are usually planned well in advance by most business owners, the historical patterns are more readily determined and easier to correlate to the level of sales activity. In the case of the ABC Company, the business owner considered his present level of insurance coverage adequate. I suggested that a complete reassessment of insurance needs and costs of current premiums was in order before establishing a projected trend line. On the basis of this recommendation, ABC Company had its insurance needs reviewed by three other carriers. This resulted in ABC cancelling its current policies and combining all its insurance with one underwriter for less cost and improved coverages.

The savings in premiums proved substantial in the first three months (Exhibit 4-9). January was $100 under the in-

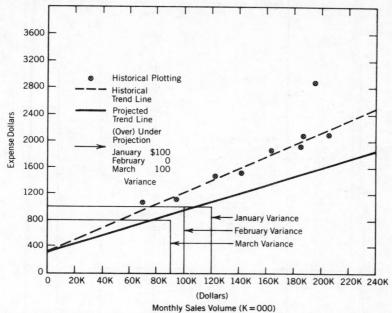

EXHIBIT 4-9.   ABC Company Insurance Expense Chart

itial projection, February $-0- under, and March $100 under. No change was made to the existing projection.

Professional Fees

This expense control included professional fees such as attorneys, accountants, and consultants. As shown in Exhibit 4-10, January was over projection by $50, February by $100, and March by $150. ABC expected the projection to hold without further change.

Interest Expense

The ABC Company was currently paying interest of two points over the prime rate on a conventional bank loan with a four-year pay back. The loan was in its first year. All ABC

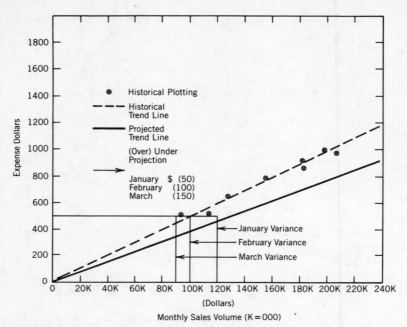

EXHIBIT 4-10.   ABC Company Professional Fees Expense Chart

payments had been on time and the principal was expected to be repaid on time. Furthermore, no additional monies were expected to be needed to support the following year's activity.

The first three months showed January and March at breakeven with February only slightly over projection by $50. No changes were made to the projection (Exhibit 4-11).

Advertising Expense

This expense is usually closely related to sales activity. However, ABC Company had anticipated an increase in this item to cover the additional monies needed to support new sales projections for the coming year. The first quarter of actual results in the exhibit supported this contention (Exhibit 4-12). January exceeded the projection by $50, February by $900, and March by $650.

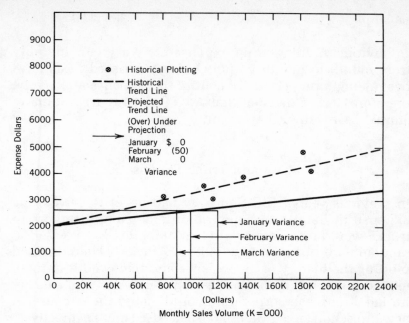

EXHIBIT 4-11.   ABC Company Interest Expense Chart

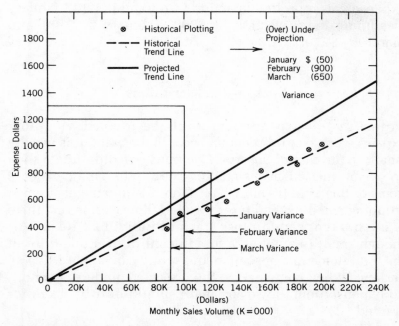

EXHIBIT 4-12.   ABC Company Advertising Expense Chart

67

Obviously, advertising expense can vary considerably from month to month without being necessarily excessive over a long-term period. To control this expense effectively, therefore, it was decided that ABC Company treat it on an annual basis rather than monthly.

Auto and Truck Expense

In previous years, ABC Company had never reviewed this expense in detail. Although maintenance and repairs to trucks were made continually, automobiles were leased at random with little concern for cost. After ABC had finished plotting the history of the expense and reviewed it in total, moratorium over any further leasing of cars was immediately initiated until the corporation could justify the expense. A new projection target was established based on this directive.

First quarter results indicated that the control over this expense was a profitable action (see Exhibit 4-13). January was under the projection by $200, February by $100, and March by $270.

Dues and Subscriptions

Ordinarily this expense item would be grouped with other expenses in a control program because the amount is usually small; in the case of the ABC Company, we did initiate such an overall miscellaneous control category to handle expense items of this kind (Exhibit 4-14). The rule to remember when grouping small expenditures together, however, is that there is often a tendency to lose track of individual items. Although small in amount, a loss in control over one-third of the total items in a miscellaneous group can create a sizable variance when compared to the projected amount. In short, no expense item, however small, should ever be taken for granted.

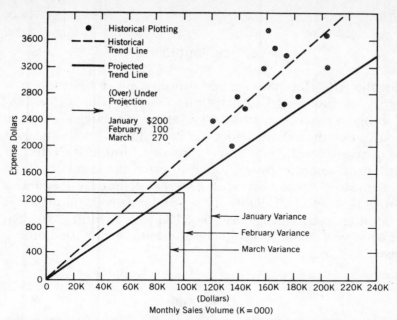

EXHIBIT 4-13.   ABC Company Auto and Truck Expense Chart

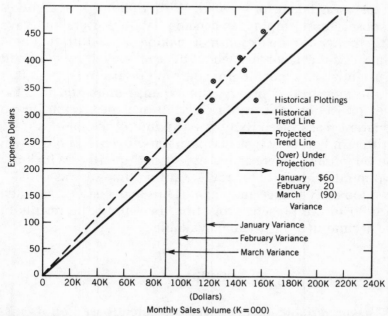

EXHIBIT 4-14.   ABC Company Dues and Subscriptions Expense Chart

Office Supplies

For the ABC Company, office supplies are in the same category as dues and subscriptions when it comes to establishing an expense control. The item is not large enough to warrant continual attention, but it is significant enough not to be overlooked. With ABC Company, I found the effect of initiating a control was enough to bring the expense down to a more acceptable amount. As a result, January was under projection by $350, February was a breakeven month, and March exceeded projection by $175 (see Exhibit 4-15). No change was made to the projected amount for the coming year.

Telephone

In the ABC Company, the use of the telephone, regardless of cost, was taken for granted. With a phone at everyone's disposal, most employees became habitual users and gave little thought to the expense of making calls. With this type of attitude prevalent throughout the company, it was difficult to establish any meaningful control. For example, note that in the month of February, the expense increased to $350 over projection and in March $150 over projection for no apparent reason (see Exhibit 4-16). Interoffice memos were written in February instructing all employees to hold down the telephone expenses for the second quarter. With only two months' activity for review at this time, it was considered too early to pass judgment. Thus, a decision was made to hold to the present projection level until the results of the second quarter became available.

Utilities

This semivariable expense was projected (based on its historical trend line) to remain fairly constant. Only February

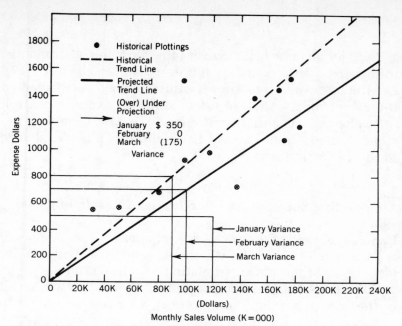

EXHIBIT 4-15. ABC Company Office Supplies Expense Chart

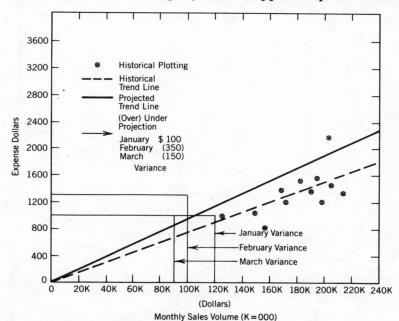

EXHIBIT 4-16. ABC Company Telephone Expense Chart

showed an increase of $225 over projection; the other months in the first quarter came in at breakeven (see Exhibit 4-17).

Although some reduction in this expense was expected from the simple action of establishing an expense control, little change was anticipated unless the ABC Company decided to relocate or expand its facilities. Thus, no change in the projection was made.

Operating Supplies and Purchases of Resale Material

I will cover both of these variable expenses under one heading because of their similar nature from an expense point of view and their close correlation to sales activity.

Both items represent large expenditures. If you will recall in the case of a group control effort, we assigned one indi-

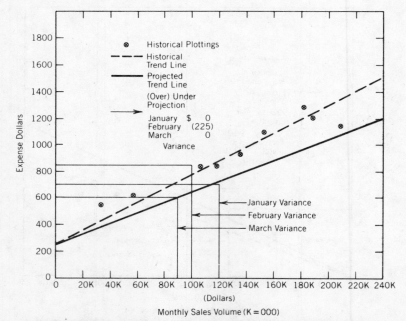

EXHIBIT 4-17.   ABC Company Utilities Expense Chart

vidual with the responsibility for keeping track of the total expenses as they were being generated throughout the month. This approach was necessary for purchasing resale material because there were so many people adding to the expense that the combined effort of the group was the only effective way of maintaining control. A similar approach was made with operating supplies.

Of the two expenses, purchasing resale material was more difficult to control because of the extended lead time required by vendors and the close correlation that existed between inventory levels and purchases. Consequently, purchasing received almost as much attention as the sales projection, with special activity paid to vendor performance. ABC's effort to control purchases during the first quarter showed promise. However, January and February were over projection by $15,000 and $10,000 respectively. But, March indicated that ABC's efforts were beginning to show results. Although the projected purchases showed $55,000, it was decided to accept the trend line as being more realistic. Therefore, Exhibit 4-4 shows $50,000 as an adjusted target and Exhibit 4-18 (which reflects a $5,000 variance under the projected trend and no variance under the historical trend) was not taken into consideration for projecting a variance for March.

On the other hand, operating supplies were more erratic (see Exhibit 4-18). January was under projection by $2000, and February and March were over projection by $2500 and $1000 respectively. Given the erratic changes during the first quarter, it was agreed that on an overall basis no change in projection could be made until the long-term effect of these changes could be reviewed.

Travel

Travel is an expense, like advertising, which does not always vary directly with sales activity. This is especially true in the case of the ABC Company because both expenses are

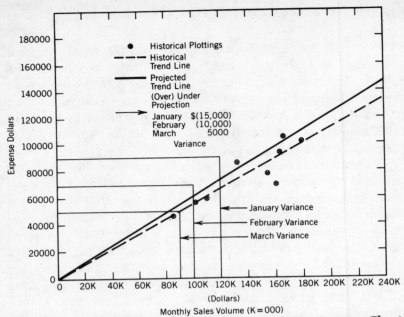

EXHIBIT 4-18. ABC Company Operating Supplies Expense Chart

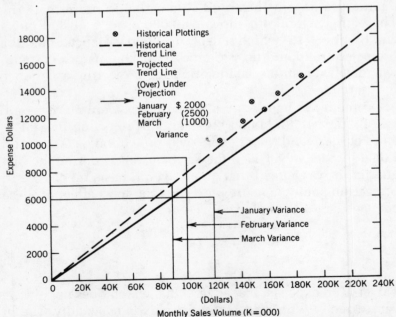

EXHIBIT 4-19. ABC Company Purchasers of Resale Material Expense Chart

often incurred prior to any increase in sales activity, causing the expense to reflect an untrue variance before the sales activity has increased. For example, ABC found it necessary to increase travel over expected levels (that would normally correlate to sales) in order to support an expanded sales program. Potential markets cannot be reached without additional travel. Closer relations with customers required more travel to customers' facilities to see what changes were being considered by the customer that might have a direct effect on ABC's marketing plans. Therefore, the travel expense projection was established at higher levels than the recorded historical trend line.

In the first quarter, actual results stayed under the projected amounts with the exception of February, which showed an increase of $2500 over projection (see Exhibit 4-20). Thus, on an overall basis the actual results, anticipated

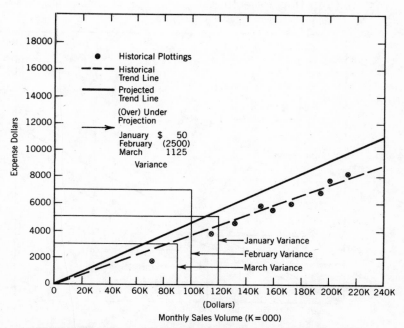

EXHIBIT 4-20.   ABC Company Travel Expense Chart

to be greater, averaged fairly close to projected levels. No change was made to the existing projection.

Uniforms

This profit and loss expense is similar to dues and subscriptions and would normally be considered part of a group of small expense items. But ABC decided to separate this item in order to monitor actual results compared to initial projection. Although small in amount, the projected amount was increased over its historical trend line. This action was considered necessary in view of the decision to provide work clothes for all employees. It was felt that this benefit might lift company morale and increase productivity.

First quarter results were considered inconclusive when compared to projected levels (see Exhibit 4-21). No change was made in the projection.

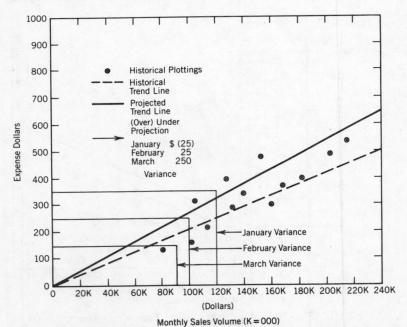

EXHIBIT 4-21.   ABC Company Uniforms Expense Chart

Entertainment

Along with travel and advertising, this expense was increased to meet the expanded sales activity. Because travel and entertainment are so closely allied, increasing one without the other would be impossible.

The first quarter showed an increase in entertainment expenses in January over projected levels of $250 and in February of $1750, which corresponds to some degree to the increase in travel expenses for the same months (see Exhibit 4-22). ABC decided to keep projection levels at the same amount until more results could be examined.

Contract Services

Contract services constitute payments made for outside assistance. In the case of the ABC Company, it combined the

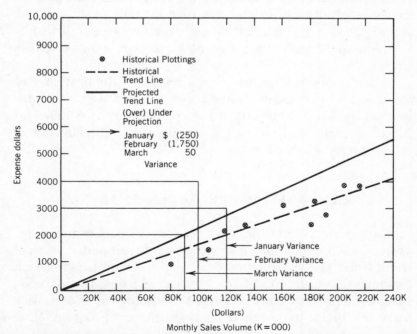

EXHIBIT 4-22.   ABC Company Entertainment Expense Chart

fees of professionals with payments made to subcontractors for specialized work needed to complete various parts for components and general outside cleaning and maintenance services. Over the past several years, the contract services expenses had shown a scattered historical pattern, which supports the basic contention that sales volume is not always a suitable indicator for controlling this particular expense item. Of all expenses placed under control by the ABC Company, subcontracting was perhaps the most difficult to correlate to any particular index. However, the task of searching for a better index than sales volume would not have been practical.

In developing an expense control projection, it is possible that you will come across an expense item that will not correlate well with sales activity or that may have a more direct correlation to another index. When this happens, many business owners consider the possibility of changing their index from sales to another index in order to correlate the expense activity better. This can be done but is not practical. *All expense controls must be measured by one index to be comparable to each other. The most acceptable index is sales activity.*

In this expense item, the actual results of the first quarter for the ABC Company showed that January was over projection by $100, February under projection by $550, and March over projection by $475 (see Exhibit 4-23). No change in the projection was made.

ACTION STEP 3: BREAKEVEN ANALYSIS

In the previous section, we saw how ABC Company reviewed each profit and loss expense, developed historical trend lines, and established a projection trend line for each expense that correlated to the projected sales. In this way, the total expense control indexed to various sales activities became a major tool of the cash management program. Now

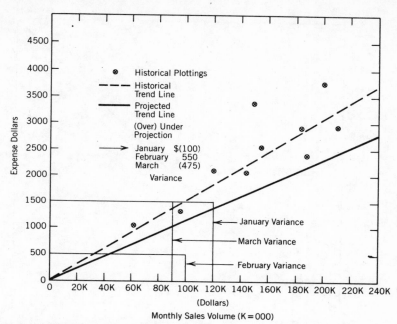

EXHIBIT 4-23. ABC Company Contractual Services Expense Chart

we will examine how the breakeven chart plays a major role in reflecting changes in sales projections and variances in expense controls by providing the final benchmark, *profitability*.

But first we must understand how to properly develop a breakeven chart (see Exhibit 4-24). One must first draw a right angle graph with equal values on both the vertical and horizontal axes. If you connect the expense line with a point on the sales line of the same value, you will have a perfect square with the same expense amount and the same sales volume. The second step is to draw a 45° line from zero sales activity to a point that represents the same sales and expense amount. And the final step is to plot the actual performance of a company, showing the total expenses generated by the business at various sales volumes. By connecting

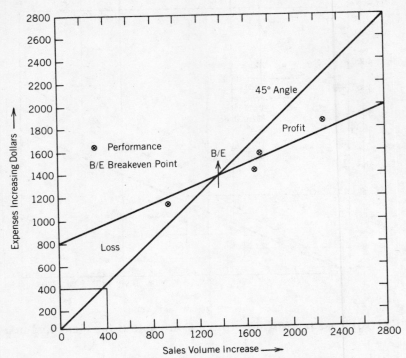

EXHIBIT 4-24.   Breakeven Chart

these points you will develop a trend line that will enable
you to determine the profit and loss performance of a business at various levels of sales volume.

Note that the trend line is much flatter than the 45° line
drawn in the previous step. The reason for this flatter slope
is the fact that actual performance reflects a mixture of fixed,
variable, and semivariable expenses, whereas a 45° line reflects a total variable correlation to sales without allowing
for fixed expenses, which, of course, is completely unrealistic. Thus, in Exhibit 4-24, expense in the amount of $800
at zero sales activity represents total fixed expenses for the
ABC Company before any sales are made. The point where

the two trend lines intersect is the breakeven point—in this example, $1,400—which is the point at which profits equal zero.

Before actual results can be posted onto the breakeven chart, let's review the results of the ABC Company more closely for the first quarter of operations. As shown in Exhibit 4-4, ABC had a total loss of $13,050 for the quarter, which is the sum of the net profit in January of $14,550 and in February of $500, less the loss in March of $28,100. Compare this to the adjusted projections for the first quarter.

In January the ABC Company dropped $10,000 in sales volume from a projected $130,000 to an actual sales volume of $120,000, (see Exhibits 4-3 and 4-4) resulting in a net profit of $14,550. The initial projection called for a net profit of $7300. Did the ABC Company realize a cash gain of $7250 ($14,550 less $7,300) in net profits on a sales volume loss of $10,000? The answer is yes, but this is only one part of the total story. The crucial question ought to be: how much damage was done to future cash reserves? Let me show you.

If you carefully reexamine Exhibit 4-4, you will note the actual ending inventory increased during the first quarter. The opening inventory in January was $20,000. By the end of January it had increased to $70,000 and by the end of February to $110,000. It ended in March with a balance of $100,000. During this same period, the sales volume was decreasing from $120,000 in January to $100,000 in February and to $90,000 in March. The effect of these two results happening concurrently was to place a severe strain on available cash. *In effect, profits were being reduced by a drop in sales volume, but the expected cash losses in profits were being deferred by allowing the level of inventory to increase.*

Let me illustrate the effect on profits when inventory is allowed to increase (see Exhibit 4-25). At first glance ABC's gross profit appears healthy, indicating a total of $171,000 in three months despite the drop in sales. Over the three-month period, how much profit would ABC have made if

EXHIBIT 4-25. ABC Company, First Quarter Monthly Projection of Gross Profits to Actual Gross Profits

	January	February	March
Net Sales	$115,000	$ 97,000	$ 89,000
Cost of Sales:			
Opening Inventory	20,000	70,000	110,000
Purchases of Resale Material	90,000	70,000	50,000
Total	110,000	140,000	160,000
Less Ending Inventory	70,000	110,000	160,000
Total Cost of Sales	40,000	30,000	60,000
Gross Profit	$ 75,000	$ 67,000	$ 29,000
Three Months Total Gross Profit			$171,000

Effect of Inventory Increase on Restricting Cash Funds:

Opening Inventory January	$ 20,000
Ending Inventory March	160,000
Cash Value of Unsold Inventory	$140,000

the ending inventory had not increased from January? Let's review Exhibit 4-26 to see the effect on profits if the ending inventory in January remained constant.

As you can see by comparing Exhibits 4-25 and 4-26, the simple act of maintaining control over the level of inventory would have increased cash funds by $90,000 ($140,000 in Exhibit 4-25 less $50,000 in Exhibit 4-26). Furthermore, gross profits were reduced in total to a more realistic amount of $141,000 ($171,000 in Exhibit 4-25 compared to $141,000 in Exhibit 4-26). What lessons have we learned from this analysis? For one thing, the profit and loss results for the ABC Company were drastically affected by a balance sheet item (ending inventory), and this despite their efforts in the area of sales and expense, which are considered by most financial professionals to be the two major determining factors in achieving profits. Secondly, you should now have a better understanding of how important the interrelationship between the profit and loss and the balance sheet areas of your cash management program can be.

Before we post the first quarter results onto the breakeven chart, it is important that you not only understand the evaluation we just discussed with respect to the first quarter but also the total financial consequences of ABC's results in the first quarter. Without the benefit of an adjusted projection to compare against actual results, most business owners would have posted only the actual results for January, February, and March. If we consider the adjusted projection to actual sales volume, we now have a different set of results to post. Furthermore, we can now consider the initial projection made by the ABC Company, amounting to $7300 profit each month on a sales volume of $130,000, to be unattainable.

In short, we now have three different profit results to consider. Which one should we post onto the breakeven chart? All three should be posted for different reasons. The initial projection when posted to the breakeven chart represents ABC's objectives, even though it is doubtful the objectives

EXHIBIT 4-26. ABC Company, First Quarter Monthly Projection of Gross Profits to Actual Gross Profits After Adjusted Inventory

	January	February	March
Net Sales	$115,000	$ 97,000	$ 89,000
Cost of Sales:			
Opening Inventory	20,000	70,000	70,000
Purchases of Resale Material	90,000	70,000	50,000
Total	110,000	140,000	120,000
Less Ending Inventory	70,000	70,000	70,000
Total Cost of Sales	40,000	70,000	50,000
Gross Profit	$ 75,000	$ 27,000	$ 39,000
Three Months Total Gross Profit			$141,000

Effect of Inventory Increase on Restricting Cash Funds:

Opening Inventory January	$ 20,000
Ending Inventory March	70,000
Cash Value of Unsold Inventory	$ 50,000

can be achieved. When the ABC Company permitted the sales volume to drop from $390,000 to $310,000 in the first quarter, it was necessary to determine if they could sustain this drop in sales volume by reducing expenses to offset the loss. Posting these results, which represents the adjusted sales and expense activity, on the breakeven chart becomes a benchmark to determine the effect on expense resulting from reduced sales activity.

The final posting shows the effect of both the sales drop in volume and the expense adjustment compared to the actual results. This posting is necessary to determine if the ABC Company is in trouble from its drop in sales and to show the effect the reduction in level of sales will have on expenses.

As posted in Exhibit 4-27, our initial sales projection and expense level gave the ABC Company a breakeven point of $92,500. This means that all monthly sales volumes below $92,500 would result in a loss and all monthly sales volume above $92,500 would generate a profit. From an objective standpoint there is no doubt the ABC Company would be comfortable with this breakeven benchmark. However, breakeven points can change quickly. As you can see by examining Exhibit 4-28, when we posted the results of our adjusted expense projection to actual sales levels, the breakeven for January was $72,000, for February it increased to $127,000, and for March it would be impossible to ever break even if the sales loss continued at its present level with the same amount of fixed expenses. In Exhibit 4-29, where we posted the actual results, the breakeven points indicated the same conditions. January showed a breakeven at $72,000, February increased to $100,000, and March results were so poor that the breakeven point would be impossible to attain.

There are several lessons to be gained in reviewing the results of these exhibits.

1. Breakeven points change monthly. The owner should look for *gradual* trends in the breakeven point of his

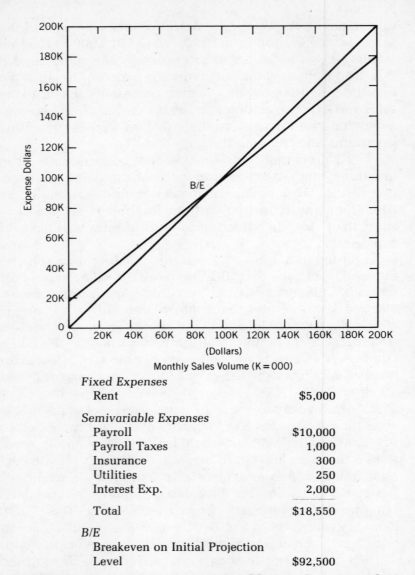

Fixed Expenses	
Rent	$5,000

Semivariable Expenses	
Payroll	$10,000
Payroll Taxes	1,000
Insurance	300
Utilities	250
Interest Exp.	2,000
Total	$18,550

B/E
Breakeven on Initial Projection
Level $92,500

EXHIBIT 4-27. ABC Company Monthly Breakeven Analysis Based on Initial Projections

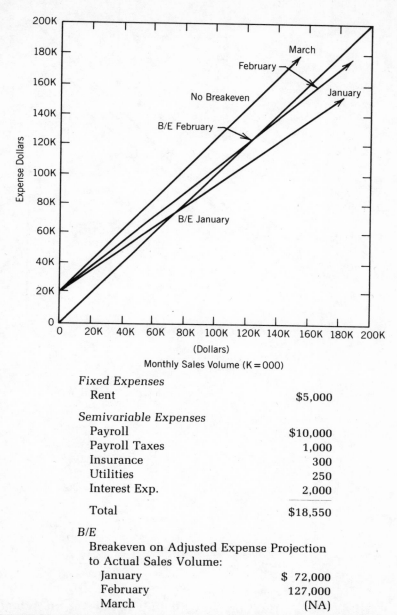

Fixed Expenses	
Rent	$5,000

Semivariable Expenses	
Payroll	$10,000
Payroll Taxes	1,000
Insurance	300
Utilities	250
Interest Exp.	2,000
Total	$18,550

B/E

Breakeven on Adjusted Expense Projection
to Actual Sales Volume:

January	$ 72,000
February	127,000
March	(NA)

**EXHIBIT 4-28. ABC Company Monthly Breakeven Analysis
Based on Adjusted Projection for Sales and Expenses**

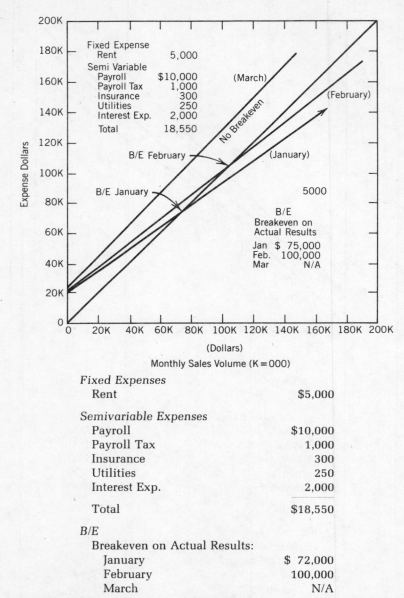

Monthly Sales Volume (K = 000)

Fixed Expenses	
Rent	$5,000
Semivariable Expenses	
Payroll	$10,000
Payroll Tax	1,000
Insurance	300
Utilities	250
Interest Exp.	2,000
Total	$18,550

B/E
Breakeven on Actual Results:

January	$ 72,000
February	100,000
March	N/A

EXHIBIT 4-29. ABC Company Monthly Breakeven on Actual

      operation rather than move too quickly to reverse any one month's activity which could easily correct itself the following month.

2.   A breakeven point that continues to increase over several months should be taken by the business owner as a warning that an immediate assessment of his or her profit and loss controls is necessary. Sales may be on the decline while expenses are increasing. Whatever the cause, the business owner must move quickly to correct the current trend, especially in the small business community where financial changes happen all too fast.

3.   A continual review of the breakeven point by the business owner and a thorough assessment of the causes is the final safety net the business owner has in the profit and loss area to prevent his or her operations from becoming one of the 9 out of 10 new businesses that fail each year.

Before proceeding further with the case history of ABC Company, let's reexamine what we have learned about our cash management program to this point. As you remember, we started with a sales projection of $390,000 in the first quarter, which dropped to $310,000 by March. Next we established a flexible expense control to provide ABC with targeted expenses at all levels of sales activities. Then we reviewed the first quarter results for the ABC Company. The sales activity had dropped from an initial $130,000 to $120,000 for the month of January. That was still well within the acceptable range of our initial sales projection. However, in February, the sales declined further to a level of $100,000 and in March they dropped to a mere $90,000—far below acceptable levels. This sales decline raised some serious questions as to whether ABC Company could sustain the continued decline. Consequently, February and March were reviewed by the sales department, which felt the trend was only a temporary slump that would correct itself the follow-

ing quarter and required no adjustments in the initial sales projections.

Practically, an owner may not be able to write off two months of sales slump as temporary. Many owners find it necessary to make immediate adjustments in their sales projections several times before the fiscal year ends. If each adjustment results in a downward trend, the only alternative is severe cuts in expenses. At ABC, the sales department had to intensify its efforts for the second quarter. Sales for the next quarter would not automatically increase without a concerted effort.

As you can see, without expense controls as an eventual backstop, sales activity targets could be continually cut to a point where the business would cease to exist. Thus without expense controls, sales projections would have no purpose.

In glancing through the expense control charts for the first quarter once again (Exhibits 4-5 through 4-23), note that in some cases expenses failed to drop along with the drop in sales, while in other cases expenses dropped below projected levels. This contrast was caused by ABC's delay in taking action. The cash management program was in place, but an attitude of complacency prevailed throughout the company. The following actions *should* have been implemented before the end of January:

1. Variable and semivariable expenses should have been reviewed *during* the month in order to put a cap on various expenses *before* they exceeded acceptable levels.

2. If the variances became excessive before the end of the month, the item should have been analyzed to determine if the expense was too high or the target level unrealistic.

3. Changes in projections for sales or expenses should have been approved after the effect on the company's breakeven was known.

4. Expense controls should have been provided as a backstop for declining sales activity. Breakeven levels provide the final backstop for both sales and expense projections.

5. Finally, adjustments to initial projections required reasonable support. In short, sales projections should not have been allowed to be continually adjusted downward, and expense targets allowed to increase, without a justifiable cause.

For a business owner, correcting the course behind the variance is the first priority; changing the projection is simply not enough. The ABC Company, however, handled its expense variances badly. For example, ABC's purchases exceeded projection by $15,000 in January, $10,000 in February, and finally showed a gain of $5,000 and a breakeven on a historical target in March. Based on only one good month's performance no changes were made in the expense projection. The gain in January of $2,000 in operating supplies was reversed by a loss of $2,500 in February and $1,000 in March. Under these circumstances, ABC Company should have tightened commitments over operating supplies in view of the poor performance in February and March. However, once again, no action was taken.

Excessive variances in payroll also needed to be reviewed in light of other increasing expenses and the declining sales activity. But ABC Company considered the problem only temporary, resulting from a decline in sales. Two steps should have been taken:

1. Reexamination of the existing employee productivity.
2. An immediate 10 percent cut of the present workforce.

The first quarter results in the profit and loss area of the cash management program for the ABC Company resulted in deep cuts into its existing cash reserves. A quick turnaround was not only needed but mandatory. If April did not show substantial improvements in both sales and expenses, cuts would have to be made immediately to protect the weakened working capital position of the company.

ACTION STEP 4: CASH SOURCES AND DISBURSEMENTS

Additional cash can be generated from many areas. The most common source known to small business owners is, of course, profits. There are, however, other sources of additional cash funds, some of which arise directly from good operating practices. Examples of this type of action results in additional interest earned from surplus cash property invested in monetary funds, or steps taken to increase the funds collected from accounts receivable. Sometimes cash can be generated as the results of *poor* operating performance as well. For example, suppose cash reserves were increased by allowing the total amount of money held in accounts payable to increase. In other words, suppose the business owner discontinues paying bills. Cash generated under these conditions is somewhat like exchanging one problem for another. Obviously, cash is accumulated when bills are not paid, but how long can a business survive without paying its suppliers? Additional cash can be acquired through the sale of company stock, but this practice causes dilution of existing shareholder's equity, a condition most shareholders would not condone. Thus, in the acquisition of additional cash, remember that some cash funds are generated from the results of actions taken by the business owner out of desperation.

Cash disbursements suffer an identity problem when compared to profit and loss expense items. The expense items reviewed up to this point are all deductible from sales income. There are other cash disbursements that are not deductible from sales income and, therefore, have *no effect* on business profits but require payment out of cash funds. For example, expenditures for operating supplies are deductible from sales income, whereas the total purchase price of a new piece of machinery cannot be deducted from sales income in the same year it is acquired. Cash is reduced in both cases; the major difference is that expenditures for items that have no useful life after one year can be expensed in that year, whereas expenditures for equipment and other related items that have a life greater than one year must be depreciated over their useful life. Thus, depreciation is an expense deduction taken each year from sales income over the life of those tangible items that can be classified as assets.

Let's examine the results of the ABC Company's first quarter opening balance sheet compared to its first quarter projected balance sheet (see Exhibit 4-30). The exhibit shows in the first column the actual opening balance at the beginning of the first quarter compared to the adjusted projected balance sheet in the second column, and the third column which shows the results at the end of the quarter. ABC Company forecasted an increase in total assets of $45,000 ($175,000 to $220,000), predicated on an increase in cash of $10,000, an increase in accounts receivable of $5,000, an increase in inventory on hand of $30,000, and the acquisition of additional equipment of $15,000 less $15,000 of depreciation write-off for the first year.

Total liabilities were also projected to increase from $120,000 to $138,000 ($18,000 increase). The net result of this increase was an increase in accounts payable of $23,000 less a reduction in the existing bank loan of $5,000.

Since assets less liabilities equal net worth, ABC's net worth in the opening balance sheet was $55,000 ($175,000 of total assets less $120,000 of total liabilities = $55,000). The projected balance sheet indicated a net worth of $82,000 at the end of the first quarter of operations ($220,000 of total assets less $138,000 of total liabilities = $82,000). Net worth in the first quarter resulted from an additional shareholders'

EXHIBIT 4-30. ABC Company Balance Sheet, First Quarter

	January First Quarter Actual Ending Balance Sheet	First Quarter Projected Balance Sheet Ending March 31st	First Quarter Actual Balance Sheet Ending March 31st
Assets			
Cash on Hand	$ –0–	$ 10,000	$ 2,000
Accounts Receivable	30,000	35,000	15,000
Inventory on Hand	20,000	50,000	100,000
Equipment	125,000	140,000	140,000
Less Depreciation	–0– $125,000	15,000 $125,000	15,000 $125,000
Total Assets	$175,000	$220,000	$242,000
Liabilities and Net Worth			
Accounts Payable	40,000	63,000	77,720
Bank Loans	80,000	75,000	75,000
Total Liabilities	$120,000	$138,000	$152,720
Net Worth			
Capital Stock	1,000	1,000	1,000
Shareholder Investment	40,000	45,100	90,000
Tax Adjustment	–0–	(450)	(2,670)
Retained Earnings	14,000	36,350	950
Total Net Worth	$ 55,000	$ 82,000	$ 89,280
Total Liabilities and Net Worth	$175,000	$220,000	$242,000

investment of $5,100 and additional earnings during the first quarter of $21,900 ($36,350 retained earnings less $450 adjustment, less opening retained earnings of $14,000).

The actual results from the balance sheet in the first quarter of operations (shown in the third column) were not quite as could have been expected when compared to the projected balance sheet. Total assets increased from $220,000 to $242,000, a $22,000 cash increase over projected assets. On the surface this increase of $22,000 would have been considered a favorable sign of good operating performance. However, closer examination of the cash funds that contributed revealed that the total assets of ABC Company were actually increased on the basis of *poor* performance. Cash on hand declined from $10,000 to $2,000, a loss of $8,000. On the other hand, accounts receivable decreased from a projected $35,000 to $15,000, a loss of available funds of $20,000. Inventory on hand was allowed to double from the projected $50,000 to a high of $100,000, providing additional funds of $50,000. The result was $50,000 of additional funds, less losses of $8,000 and $20,000: net $22,000.

Little gratification can be taken from such an increase in assets. As previously discussed, not all increases in cash funds automatically mean good performance. If anything, the ABC Company had created future problems by allowing its liquid cash to deplete through the reduction of its current accounts receivable and by allowing the level of inventory to increase to an extremely high level. Furthermore, little was done to reduce ABC's total liabilities, which increased to $152,720 for a total increase over projection of $14,720 ($152,700 less $138,000). Consequently, the actual net worth of the ABC Company at the end of the first quarter was $89,280, an increase over projection of $7,280. Thus, total assets increased as a result of poor performance rather than through effective control over cash funds. An increase in liabilities resulting from lack of control by ABC resulted in an increase in net worth, not from retained earnings but from additional influx of capital funds from various shareholders of $44,900 ($90,000 less $45,100).

The application of cash funds by the ABC Company for the first quarter reflects a total disregard of cash funds shown on the balance sheet (see Exhibit 4-31). Inventory increased to $80,000 from a projected $30,000, a $50,000 loss of cash! No attempt was made to curtail the initial projection to buy additional equipment of $15,000, which reflects a total disregard by ABC of what had already happened to the cash reserves on the balance sheet.

The end result of all this activity during the first quarter was the reduction of cash on hand to a mere $2,000. Furthermore, ABC would have gone under had it not been for the shareholders' investment of $50,000.

In just three short months, ABC managed to lose sales, overrun its projected expenses, and finally, fail to curtail its application of funds on the balance sheet in view of what was certainly a sagging source of available cash.

Despite the fact that ABC Company had established projections and initiated expense controls, it failed to stay within the limits of its projections and execute its controls. An acceptable breakeven, which serves as a benchmark to gauge the sales and expense activity and provide acceptable working capital levels, went unnoticed. There were steps, however, that could have been initiated to correct the poor performance. Accounts receivable fell because ABC allowed bookings to drop, causing an immediate need for cash which pressured the accelerated collection of existing accounts receivable. Thus, it came as no surprise that accounts payable increased because of ABC's lack of cash to pay its vendors. Purchases for resale material should have been curtailed well below projected levels and a program to sell off obsolete inventory should have been started. Equipment purchases, along with inventory purchases, should have been curtailed. The failure to do this resulted in further drains on already slim cash reserves. The action on the part of the shareholders

EXHIBIT 4-31. ABC Company Application of Cash Funds, First Quarter

Projected First Quarter

Cash Sources		
Net Income (from Profit and Loss)		$ 21,900
Other Sources of Cash		
Depreciation	$15,000	
Accounts Payable Increase	23,000	
Shareholders Investment	5,100	43,100
Total Cash Sources		$ 65,000
Application of Cash Funds		
Accounts Receivable Increase	$ 5,000	
Inventory Increase	30,000	
Equipment Purchases	15,000	
Bank Loan Payments	5,000	
Total Application of Funds		$(55,000)
Cash on Hand Increase		$ 10,000[a]
[a]Cash on Hand	January 1st	$ –0–
Cash on Hand	March 31st	10,000
	Cash Increase	$10,000

Actual First Quarter

Cash Sources		
Net Income (from profit and loss)		$ (15,720)
Other Sources of Cash		
Accounts Receivable Decreased	$15,000	
Depreciation	15,000	
Accounts Payable Increased	37,720	
Additional Shareholders Investment	50,000	117,720
Total Cash Sources		$ 102,000
Application of Cash Funds		
Inventory Increase	$80,000	
Equipment Purchase	15,000	
Bank Loan Payment	5,000	
Total Application of Funds		$(100,000)
Cash on Hand Increase		$ 2,000[b]
[b]Cash on Hand	January 1st	$ –0–
Cash on Hand	March 31st	2,000
	Cash Increase	$ 2,000

to reinvest additional funds into ABC was a move inspired out of sheer desperation to save the company.

In summary:

1. Changes affecting the financial position within a small business happen quickly. Therefore, any time taken to make changes becomes critical to the success of any cash management program.

2. Controls should always be in place and ready to initiate when necessary.

3. Revisions in projections to meet changing conditions should be limited to what effect they will have on a company's profit and loss level of working capital.

Working capital should be thought of in terms of monies needed to operate. The working capital level must be large enough to support the business operation over a specified period of time. For some companies, that might represent a few weeks; for others it will require several months. Finally, working capital funds can be influenced by events within and outside the operation. For example, an increase or decrease in retained earnings directly affects the existing working capital level. On the other hand, an investment from a shareholder or a short-term infusion of money from a bank can also increase working capital levels. *In short, the key to operating a successful cash management program is to take all steps necessary to build a balanced program that will provide sufficient working capital.*

In the case of the ABC Company, there was no coordination between the control of profits and the control of cash. Therefore, the first mistake made by the ABC Company was to disregard the combined effect on cash when losses in the profit and loss areas are not corrected and the balance sheet items are not given proper attention at the same time. Thus, when the ABC Company was unable to meet its sales projections, it reviewed its marketing department and developed a new sales projection. When its expenses exceeded their established projections, it reviewed the various expenses, established new levels of responsibility, and capped many of the variable expenses. But these steps were taken without consideration of other factors within the cash management program—for example, Balance Sheet control—which led to additional sources of cash and the curtailment of excessive application of funds. A rule of thumb: action steps taken under a cash management program must be taken on a combined basis, taking into consideration all areas that will result in an ending balance of cash-on-hand that is sufficient to carry the company's objectives forward.

A quick statement preparation should have been made before the first quarter ended to ascertain what was happening to cash levels. In ABC's case, cash funds were all but depleted by the time it reviewed its operations. A continual drop in the ABC Company checkbook should have been enough to signal some type of action. Second, ABC should have considered what options were available had it taken an overall view, such as readjusting sales projections, variable expenses, or balance sheet disbursements. Changes in the source of funds should have been initiated, thereby easing the pressure on sales and expense controls. If the ABC Company had established its working capital level first and then reviewed its options, the task would have been much simpler and more easily identified.

Assume that the ABC Company wanted to maintain a working capital level of $35,000 at the end of the first quarter. The first area of review should have been the sources of available cash. Although the ABC Company attacked the balance of outstanding accounts receivable, it allowed its inventory to climb during reduced sales activity by continuing to buy merchandise. It is quite conceivable that had they known what was happening to purchases, one simple action to curtail further buying might have increased the ending level of cash to the extent that the balance may have been greater than the projected amount. ABC Company should have taken joint action against both inventory (a balance sheet control) and purchases (an expense control) to achieve the desired funds on hand at the end of the first quarter.

Another example of the lack of control by the ABC Company was their ineffective use of their cash management program. Was there really sudden need to request additional capital from existing shareholders? In this case, they were lucky. Most businesses have only a few shareholders, who are not likely to be so affluent or generous as to come forward with additional funds when their company has failed to control its operation. In most cases, the shareholders of a small business are more apt to ask embarassing questions and demand action to be taken to redirect the operations. The only reason the ABC Company was able to prevail on its existing shareholders was primarily because of the condition of their operations at the end of the first quarter. The ABC Company was essentially in a do-or-die situation; without the additional infusion of capital it would have collapsed.

To summarize:

1. ABC Company waited too long to assess their actual results-to-projection and therefore almost suffered a complete failure.

2. The ABC Company executed its controls to redirect operations in a piecemeal fashion, ignoring the cash sources and cash disbursements parts of the balance sheet. In other words, their actions were fragmented and ineffective.

3. Far too much reliance was placed upon assistance from the outside shareholders rather than attempting to correct the problems within.

4. Having elaborate controls in place is not a guarantee of a problem-free operation. Controls are a manage-

ment *tool* that must be used to redirect operations and allow the business to improve its level of operations. Controls that are not utilized become antiquated in the eyes of the business owner long before they become outdated.

5

THE QUICK FIX
AND FINAL CONTROL

The first quarter results for the ABC Company were a total disaster, almost leading the business to complete collapse. At this point, ABC was faced with some very difficult choices. Whatever action they decided to take had to be both effective and quickly done. Its results would have to be strong enough to overcome the poor showing in the first quarter and to place the second quarter activity back on track. Furthermore, it was obvious from the first quarter that ABC needed more than just having cash management tools available. Their failure to utilize these tools in the first quarter was evidence of a lack of appreciation for what they could do if effectively and properly used.

We finally decided that time was the most critical factor. Therefore, ABC initiated a crash program that I later labeled "quick fix" to remedy the financial problems as quickly as possible. Once this had been completed, ABC would expand their present cash management program to include supporting operational programs that would enable them to take more positive action toward the financial results to ensure more constructive and lasting results.

Let's first describe the action taken under the crash program.

ACTION STEP 1: REDIRECT THE EFFORTS OF THE SALES DEPARTMENT

As you may recall from Chapter 4, ABC initially believed that the drop in sales from January to March was only a temporary condition that would correct itself in the second quarter. I disagreed with this thinking and persuaded them to review their program and take appropriate steps to increase their level of sales. They agreed and initiated a review of their marketing policy with existing customers. After careful consideration, ABC decided to make an effort to regain the initiative with the Smith Company. As you recall, Smith had given its redesign work to one of ABC's competitors. Relying on the fact that the Smith Company had an aggressive marketing program and would act quickly to seize a better product at reduced costs, ABC directed its engineering department to initiate a crash program to redesign the product so that it would sell for less than its competitor but still be of superior quality.

Although the engineering department had revised this product once before the cost reduction, it was hoped a second review would produce better results. A unit from ABC's competitor was acquired and the engineering department began its redesign program. Within two weeks the prototype was presented to the Smith Company. It was cheaper and of better quality than ABC's former effort and far superior to the competitor's product. Although Smith reserved the right to buy from ABC's competitor, the sales and engineering effort paid off and Smith reordered. On the basis of these additional sales, April results were $110,000, May $135,000 and June $160,000; a total increase over projection of $15,000 for the second quarter (see Exhibit 5-1). In addition, sales efforts were expanded into new marketing areas that did not result in immediate bookings but did show promise for the second half of the year.

ACTION STEP 2: SALES PROMOTION OF INVENTORY ON HAND

Inventory-on-hand was carefully classified and physically counted. Items with a shelf life of more than 12 months were reduced in price and offered to various customers at a 25 percent discount. As a result, actual ending inventory dropped in May to $75,000 from an opening balance of $100,000 (see Exhibit 5-1). During the same month purchases were curtailed to $40,000 compared to an adjusted projection of $82,500. There was no visible increase in gross profits from these actions because profit margins were cut when the 25 percent discount was given to various customers. However, the level of inventory-on-hand was reduced providing additional shelf space, removing what was obsolete and allowing ABC to replenish its existing stock with new merchandise.

ACTION STEP 3: EXPENSE CONTROL

A program to control expenses began in earnest. In April, total expenses exceeded the adjusted projection by $4225 (see Exhibit 5-1 and Exhibits 5-2 through 5-20). The only major expense items that exceeded projection for the three months were advertising, travel, and entertainment. The bases for these increases were the expanded efforts in the sales department to secure new markets.

In April, the total expense was over projection by $4225; in May, by $4700; in June, by $12,005. Although advertising, travel, and entertainment increased, they were partially offset by reductions in other expenses. The most sizable reduction in this category was payroll, with an actual expense

EXHIBIT 5-1. ABC Company Profit and Loss, Second Quarter

April

	Initial Projection	Actual	Variance	Adjusted Sales and Expenses	Initial Projection
Sales	$130,000	$ 110,000	–0–	$ 110,000	$130,000
Earned Interest	5,000	5,000	–0–	5,000	5,000
Total Income	$135,000	$ 115,000	$ –0–	$ 115,000	$135,000
Less Returns	12,000	8,000	4,000	12,000	12,000
Net Income	$123,000	$ 107,000	$ (4,000)	$ 103,000	$123,000
Less Cost of Sales"	50,000	70,000	7,500	77,500	50,000
Gross Profit	$ 73,000	$ 37,000	$ 11,500	$ 25,500	$ 73,000
Less Expenses					
General Taxes	2,000	1,800			2,000
FICA Taxes	1,400	1,400	(200)	3,500	1,400
Unemployment Taxes	500	500			500
Rent	5,000	5,000	–0–	5,000	5,000
Repair and Maintenance	2,500	2,000	200	2,200	2,500
Gross Payroll	20,000	18,000	500	18,500	20,000
Insurance	1,200	1,000	75	1,075	1,200
Professional Fees	500	500	(75)	425	500
Interest Expense	2,500	2,500	(100)	2,400	2,500
Advertising	800	1,000	(325)	675	800
Auto/Truck	1,800	1,500	–0–	1,500	1,800
Dues and Subscriptions	300	200	55	255	300
Office Supplies	900	800	(50)	750	900
Telephone	1,200	1,200	(200)	1,000	1,200
Utilities	750	750	(75)	675	750
Operating Supplies	8,500	7,000	250	7,250	8,500
Travel	6,000	8,000	(3,000)	5,000	6,000
Uniforms	350	300	–0–	300	350
Entertainment	3,000	4,000	(1,500)	2,500	3,000
Contract Service	1,500	1,000	220	1,220	1,500
Total Expenses	$ 60,700	$ 58,450	$ (4,225)	$ 54,225	$ 60,700
Operating Profit	12,300	(21,450)	7,275	(28,725)	12,300
Depreciation	5,000	5,000	–0–	5,000	5,000
Net Profit	$ 7,300	$ (26,450)	$ 7,275	$ (33,725)	$ 7,300
"Cost of Sales:					
Opening Inventory	$ 20,000	$ 100,000	$ –0–	$ 100,000	$ 20,000
Purchases	80,000	60,000	7,500	67,500	80,000
Total	$100,000	$ 160,000	$ 7,500	$ 167,500	$100,000
Ending Inventory	50,000	70,000	–0–	90,000	50,000
Cost of Sales	$ 50,000	$ 70,000	$ 7,500	$ 77,500	$ 50,000

(monthly projection compared to actual)

	May			June		
Actual	Variance	Adjusted Sales and Expenses	Initial Projection	Actual	Variance	Adjusted Sales and Expenses
$135,000	$ -0-	$135,000	$130,000	$160,000	$ -0-	$160,000
5,000	-0-	5,000	5,000	5,000	-0-	5,000
$140,000	$ -0-	$140,000	$135,000	$165,000	$ -0-	$165,000
10,000	2,000	12,000	12,000	10,000	2,000	12,000
$130,000	$ 2,000	$128,000	$123,000	$155,000	$ 2,000	$153,000
55,000	2,500	52,500	50,000	75,000	16,250	58,750
$ 75,000	$ (500)	$ 75,500	$ 73,000	$ 80,000	$ 14,250	$ 94,250
1,800			2,000	1,800		
1,000	900	4,100	1,400	1,000	1,475	4,675
400			500	400		
5,000	-0-	5,000	5,000	5,000	-0-	5,000
1,800	950	2,750	2,500	1,800	1,450	3,250
16,000	4,500	20,500	20,000	16,000	6,500	22,500
1,500	(250)	1,250	1,200	1,200	220	1,420
400	125	525	500	400	225	625
2,500	-0-	2,500	2,500	2,500	100	2,600
1,500	(675)	825	800	1,500	(550)	950
1,800	100	1,900	1,800	1,500	700	2,200
250	60	310	300	250	115	365
700	230	930	900	750	350	1,100
1,300	(50)	1,250	1,200	1,200	275	1,475
700	60	760	750	700	150	850
7,500	1,500	9,000	8,500	8,000	2,500	10,500
8,000	(1,750)	6,250	6,000	8,000	(700)	7,300
300	50	350	350	300	120	420
4,500	(1,450)	3,050	3,000	5,000	(1,300)	3,700
1,200	400	1,600	1,500	1,500	375	1,875
$ 58,150	$ 4,700	$ 62,850	$ 60,700	$ 58,800	$ 12,005	$ 70,805
16,850	4,200	12,650	12,300	21,200	2,245	23,445
5,000	-0-	5,000	5,000	5,000	-0-	5,000
$ 11,850	$ 4,200	$ 7,650	$ 7,300	$ 16,200	$ 2,245	$ 18,445
$ 90,000	$ -0-	$ 90,000	$ 20,000	$ 75,000	$ 45,000	$120,000
40,000	42,500	82,500	80,000	75,000	13,750	88,750
$130,000	$ 42,500	$172,500	$100,000	$150,000	$ 58,750	$208,750
75,000	45,000	120,000	50,000	75,000	75,000	150,000
$ 55,000	$ 2,500	$ 52,500	$ 50,000	$ 75,000	$ 16,250	$ 58,750

of $18,000 in April and $16,000 in both May and June. This reduction was accomplished by requesting each department supervisor to review worker performance, which brought a series of expensive practices to light, including duplication of efforts between departments, incompetence, and inefficiency. Several employees were fired or resigned and the payroll savings in the second quarter was $11,500 (total ad-

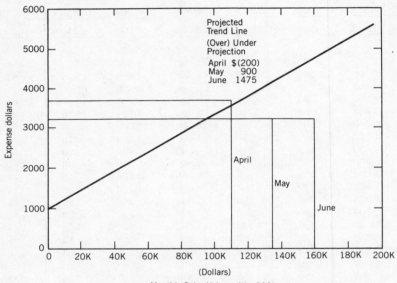

Second Quarter Actions
Taxes decreased with the adoption of a pension plan and reduction in payroll. Without the adoption of a constructive employee relations program, however, ABC will not be able to operate on the reduced level of present employees.

Projected Trend Line (Over) Under Projection:

April	$(200)
May	900
June	1,475

EXHIBIT 5-2.   ABC Company General Taxes and Payroll Taxes Expense Chart—Semivariable

justed projection for gross payroll for April, May, and June of $61,500 less actual payroll for the same period of $50,000). Other expense items were kept under control even though the individual efforts were based on desperate actions that resolved problems temporarily but with some desirable and undesirable consequences for the future (glance through Exhibits 5-2 to 5-20).

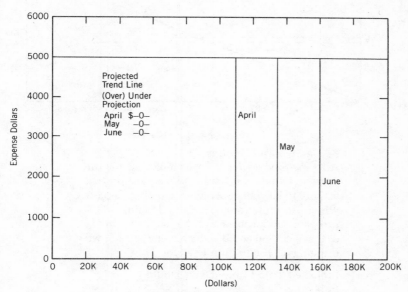

Expense Dollars

6000

5000

4000   Projected
        Trend Line
        (Over) Under
        Projection   April
        April $—0—
3000   May   —0—
        June   —0—   May

2000   June

1000

0
  0   20K   40K   60K   80K 100K 120K 140K 160K 180K 200K
                        (Dollars)
                Monthly Sales Volume (K = 000)

Second Quarter Actions
No action was taken to reduce rent. The current amount of rent is based on terms of a lease. A change in rent would require breaking the current lease arrangement and moving to new facilities. The cost of this action was considered to be more expense than the cost of the present rent.

Projected Trend Line (Over) Under
Projection:
    April $—0—
    May   —0—
    June   —0—

EXHIBIT 5-3.   ABC Company Rent Expense Chart—Fixed

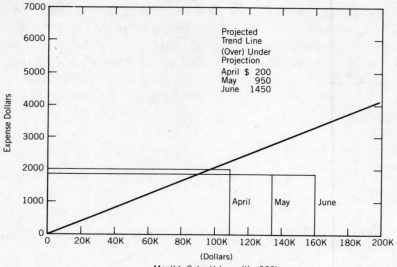

Second Quarter Actions

All repairs were temporarily deferred for the present. Maintenance was reduced to a limited activity to keep the operations growing. Repairs which are supported by a limited maintenance program cannot, however, be deferred forever or the operation could suffer a major breakdown bringing all production to a stop.

Projected Trend Line (Over) Under Projection:

April	$ 200
May	950
June	1,450

EXHIBIT 5-4.   ABC Company Repair and Maintenance Expense Chart—Variable

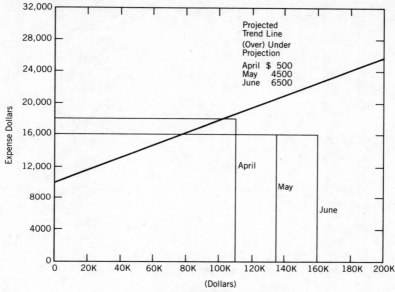

Second Quarter Actions

Reduction in the present work force will only hold if ABC adopts a constructive employee relations program.

Projected Trend Line (Over) Under Projection:

April	$ 500
May	4,500
June	6,500

EXHIBIT 5-5. ABC Company Gross Payroll Expense Chart— Semivariable

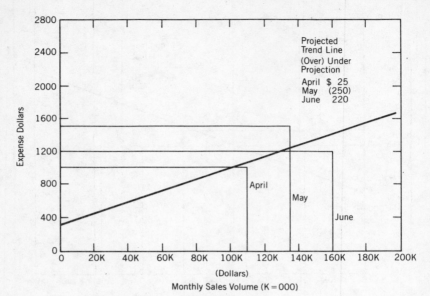

Second Quarter Actions

A permanent reduction in the cost of insurance requires the cancellation of specific insurance policies or the reduction of coverage. ABC was not ready to make the commitment and therefore no action was taken in this area.

Projected Trend Line (Over) Under Projection:

April	$ 75
May	(250)
June	220

EXHIBIT 5-6.   ABC Company Insurance Expense Chart—Semi-variable

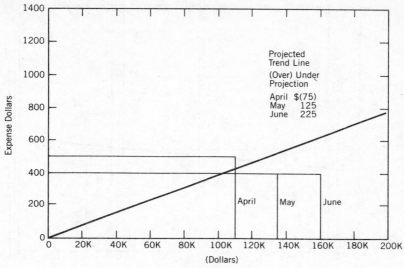

Second Quarter Actions

Given the present confusion over business activity and the possibility of failure, the last thing ABC wanted to do was to cut professional assistance. However, the professional fees decreased from April through June.

Projected Trend Line (Over) Under Projection:

April	$ (75)
May	125
June	225

EXHIBIT 5-7.   ABC Company Professional Fees Expense Chart—Variable

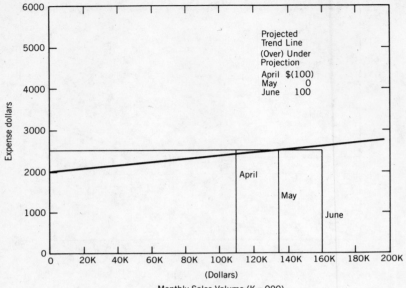

Second Quarter Actions
Interest expense was based on an existing loan which ABC has no plans at this time to reconstitute. No action taken.

Projected Trend Line (Over) Under
Projection:

April	$(100)
May	–0–
June	100

EXHIBIT 5-8. ABC Company Interest Expense Chart—Semi-variable

114

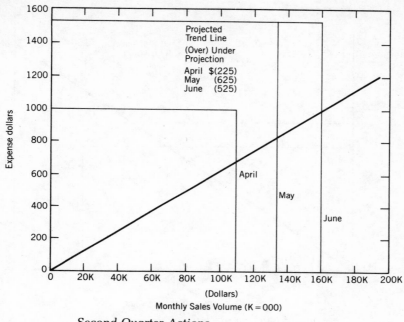

Second Quarter Actions
(Previously discussed)

Projected Trend Line (Over) Under
Projection:
April	$(225)
May	(625)
June	(525)

EXHIBIT 5-9. ABC Company Advertising Expense Chart—Variable

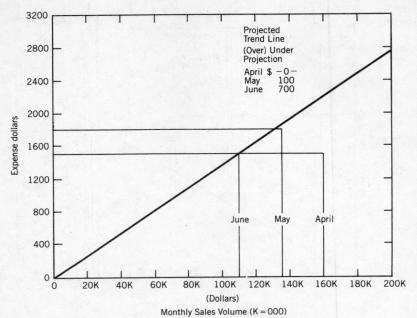

Monthly Sales Volume (K = 000)

Second Quarter Actions

The most significant reduction to this expense was the termination of lease cars for key employees and management personnel. The savings should continue, assuming no changes in personnel policies.

Projected Trend Line (Over) Under
Projection:

April	$–0–
May	100
June	700

EXHIBIT 5-10.   ABC Company Auto—Truck Expense Chart— Variable

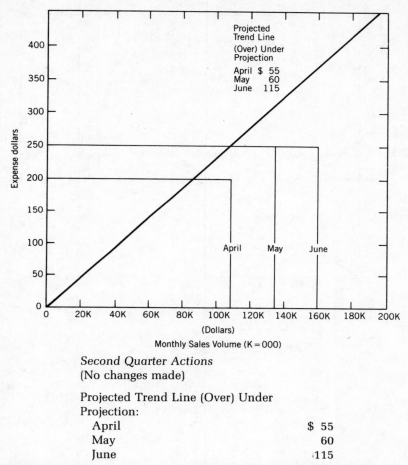

Second Quarter Actions
(No changes made)

Projected Trend Line (Over) Under
Projection:
April $ 55
May   60
June   ,115

EXHIBIT 5-11.   ABC Company Dues and Subscription Expense Chart—Variable

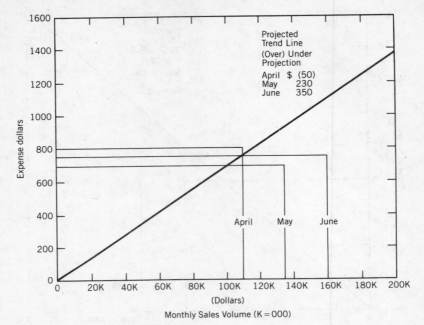

Monthly Sales Volume (K = 000)

Second Quarter Actions
A management decision to reduce the level of
office supplies on hand by curtailing purchases
are expected to hold the present level of expenses.

Projected Trend Line (Over) Under
Projection:

April	$ (50)
May	230
June	350

**EXHIBIT 5-12.   ABC Company Office Supplies Expense Chart—
Variable**

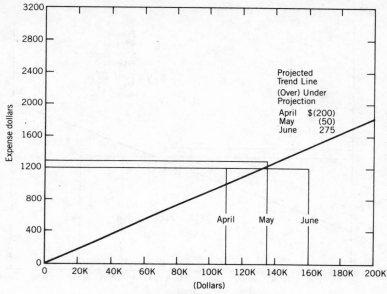

Monthly Sales Volume (K = 000)

Second Quarter Actions
Fixing the responsibility of telephone calls to specific individuals reduced the present level of expense. An education program on the proper use of the telephone is still needed.

Projected Trend Line (Over) Under
Projection:

April	($200)
May	(50)
June	275

EXHIBIT 5-13. ABC Company Telephone Expense Chart— Variable

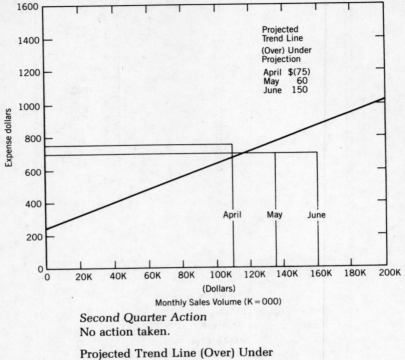

Second Quarter Action
No action taken.

Projected Trend Line (Over) Under
Projection:

April	$ (75)
May	60
June	150

EXHIBIT 5-14.   ABC Company Utilities Expense Chart—Semi-variable

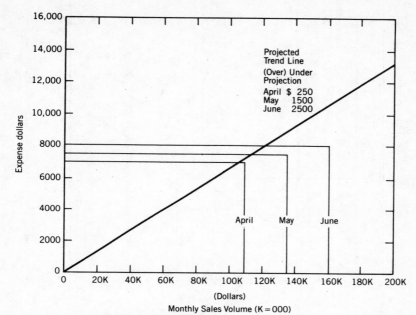

Monthly Sales Volume (K = 000)

Second Quarter Actions

All existing invoices were held for future payment until further notice. This band aid effort will not hold the line and will only add monies to new invoice currently being committed. The control point is at the time of commitment. ABC has yet to formalize this action.

Projected Trend Line (Over) Under Projection:

April	$ 250
May	1,500
June	2,500

EXHIBIT 5-15. ABC Company Operating Supplies Expense Chart—Variable

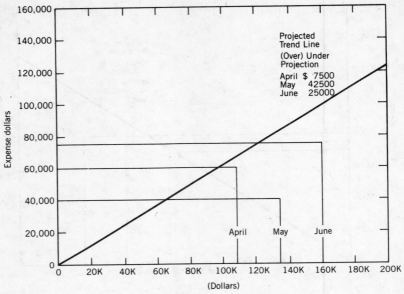

Second Quarter Action
Same action as Exhibit 5-15.

Projected Trend Line (Over) Under
Projection:

April	$ 7,500
May	42,500
June	2,500

EXHIBIT 5-16. ABC Company Purchasing of Resale Material Expense Chart—Variable

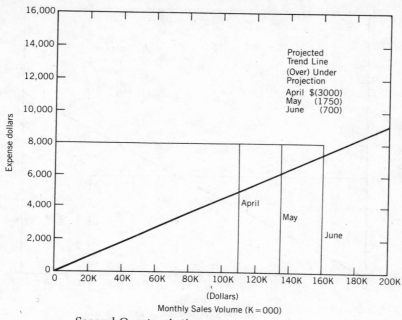

Expense dollars

Monthly Sales Volume (K = 000)
(Dollars)

Projected
Trend Line
(Over) Under
Projection

April $(3000)
May   (1750)
June   (700)

Second Quarter Action
Previously discussed.

Projected Trend Line (Over) Under
Projection:

April	$(3,000)
May	(1,750)
June	(700)

EXHIBIT 5-17.   ABC Company Travel Expense Chart—Variable

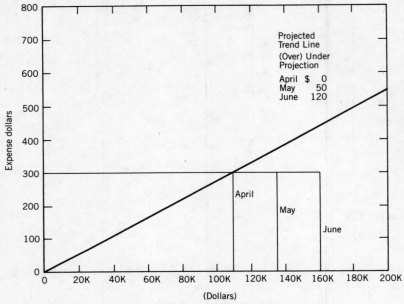

Second Quarter Action
No action taken.

Projected Trend Line (Over) Under
Projection:
April	$ -0-
May	50
June	120

EXHIBIT 5-18. ABC Company Uniforms Expense Chart—Variable

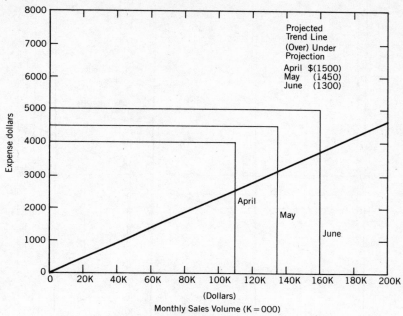

Second Quarter Action
Previously discussed.

Projected Trend Line (Over) Under
Projection:
April	$(1,500)
May	(1,450)
June	(1,300)

EXHIBIT 5-19.   ABC Company Entertainment Expense Chart—Variable

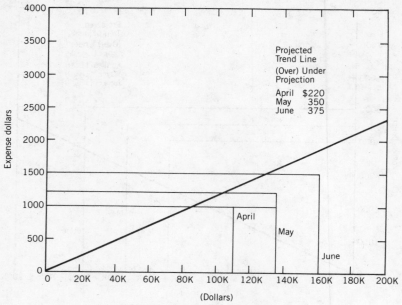

Second Quarter Actions

Where it was possible, subcontracting services were terminated and the work brought back to the ABC plant. It remained to be seen if the ABC company could do the added work just as effectively as the subcontractors at the same costs. If ABC fails to follow through on this assessment, the action may cost more money than before the work was shifted.

Projected Trend Line (Over) Under Projection:

April	$220
May	350
June	375

EXHIBIT 5-20.   ABC Company Contract Service Expense Chart— Variable

ACTION STEP 4: BALANCE SHEET CONTROL

The most significant action taken (see Exhibit 5-21) was a drop in total assets from $242,000 at the end of March to $228,050 at the end of June. Cash on hand increased from $2000 at the end of March to $23,050 by the end of June.

You will recall from the previous chapter that an increase or decrease in total assets on the balance sheet from one period to another is no guarantee that your business has experienced favorable growth in available surplus cash. However, the action taken by the ABC Company in the second quarter was more constructive when one compares the actual in March to the actual in June. Cash increased from $2,000 in March to $23,050 in June, a $21,050 increase in cash funds. But accounts receivable also increased from $15,000 in March to $20,000 in June and resulted in a $5,000 loss of cash funds; on the other hand, inventory decreased from $100,000 in March to $75,000 in June, an increase in cash funds of $25,000. Equipment net of depreciation decreased from $125,000 in March to $110,000 in June, an increase in cash funds of $15,000. As a result, total assets dropped by $13,950 ($21,050 increase in cash and $5,000 increase in Accounts Receivable, less $25,000 reduction in inventory, less a $15,000 net decrease in equipment). The total increase in available cash on hand was $21,050 ($23,050 less $2,000).

Total liabilities dropped $15,550 from March to June ($152,720 in March to $137,170 in June). The decrease was due to a reduction in accounts payable in March of $77,720 to $67,170 in June, a cash savings of $10,550, and to the payment of a $5,000 bank loan, reducing the loan in March from $75,000 to $70,000 in June.

Total net worth increased from $89,280 in March to $90,880 in June, a cash savings of $1,600 (assets loss of $13,950 less liability loss of $15,550 equals $1,600 savings).

In short, all balance sheet changes made by the ABC Company in the second quarter were positive (see Exhibit 5-22). Cash-on-hand was increased while inventory was reduced.

EXHIBIT 5-21. ABC Company Balance Sheet, Second Quarter

	March 31st Actual Ending Balance Sheet		Second Quarter Projected Balance Sheet Ending June 30th		Second Quarter Actual Balance Sheet Ending June 30th	
Assets						
Cash		$ 2,000		$ 20,000		$ 23,500
Accounts Receivable		15,000		35,000		20,000
Inventory on Hand		100,000		50,000		75,000
Equipment	140,000		140,000		140,000	
Less Depreciation	15,000	125,000	30,000	110,000	30,000	110,000
Total Assets		$242,000		$215,000		$228,050
Liabilities and Net Worth						
Accounts Payable		77,720		78,720		67,170
Bank Loan		75,000		70,000		70,000
Total Liabilities		$152,720		$148,720		$137,170
Capital Stock		1,000		1,000		1,000
Shareholder Investment		90,000		45,100		90,000
Retained Earnings		(1,720)		20,180		(120)
Total Net Worth		$ 89,280		$ 66,280		$ 90,880
Total Liabilities and Net Worth		$242,000		$215,000		$228,050

Accounts payable was reduced and the payment to the bank was made. Total net worth increased from additional profits rather than additional investments from shareholders. Thus, the ABC Company was able to initiate a crash program to redirect their cash management program at the beginning of the second quarter of the year.

The problem was difficult, however; and it would be wrong to leave you with the impression that ABC's crash program was simple to execute. First, it is important to remember that if no action had been taken prior to the second quarter, and the ABC Company would have failed at the end of the first three months if it had not been for the additional investments from shareholders. Second, you must understand that the actions taken by ABC constituted an enormous task to insure that total recovery was achieved by the end of the second quarter. Failure to act more quickly during the first quarter of the year, along with an ineffective utilization and understanding of the cash management program, shifted all the burden of correcting the results to the second quarter.

There is an important rule to remember at this point. *The purpose of a cash management program is to reflect in financial terms the success or failure of all actions taken by the business owner. Therefore, in order for a cash management program to be effective it is absolutely essential that it be supported by other control systems.* Let's examine some of these support systems in light of the action taken by the ABC Company prior to the beginning of the second quarter.

Redirect the Efforts of the Sales Department

Although the action taken with the sales department was quick and effective, in essence it only provided a "band-aid" effort for handling the immediate problem. What ABC needed to support their projected sales effort was a balanced marketing program.

EXHIBIT 5-22. ABC Company Application of Cash Funds, Second Quarter

	Projected Second Quarter	Actual Second Quarter
Cash Sources		
Net Income (from Profit & Loss)	$21,900	$ 1,600
Other Sources of Cash		
Accounts Payable Increase	1,000	
Depreciation	15,000	15,000
Inventory Decrease	50,000	25,000
	66,000	40,000
Total Cash Sources	87,900	41,600
Application of Cash Funds		
Accounts Receivable Increase	20,000	5,000
Shareholders' Investment Decrease	44,900	
Accounts Payable Decrease		10,550
Bank Loan Payment	5,000	5,000
Total Application of Funds	69,900	20,500
Cash on Hand Increase	$18,000"	$21,050"
"Cash on Hand March 31	$ 2,000	$ 2,000
Cash on Hand June 30	20,000	23,050
Cash Increase	$18,000	$21,050

In Chapter 3 I listed for you some of the essential elements of an effective sales and marketing program.

There are several techniques essential to the development of a merchandising and marketing program that ought to be considered. *The importance of this area cannot be overlooked. The life blood of any business comes from its ability to sell its products or services, and without sufficient sales, a business cannot hope to succeed.* It is, therefore, absolutely essential that you have a thorough understanding of what I mean by a merchandising and sales program which will properly support a cash management program. Let's examine some of the basic factors of sales and marketing as outlined in my recent book *The Action-Step Plan to Owning and Operating a Successful Business.*

Although many articles and books have been written on merchandising, in its simplest terms it is the ability to sell your product or service. This ability is not an inherited characteristic; it only comes from training and experience, which develop the essential requirements for a successful sales person, namely, conveying credibility about your product or service better than anyone else can. Selling succeeds only to the extent that you possess the ability to convince others you have something that they need. If you do not possess a thorough knowledge of your product or service, you will surely fail, and in this respect initial contacts with prospective customers are the most vital, since they establish the all-critical first impressions and set the tone for further customer relationships. Sales promotions are another important tool in any marketing program. There are various factors that must be considered in any merchandising and marketing program, and among them are sales promotions. Many businesses hold promotional sales of products on a yearly basis. There are good reasons for this. (1) It reduces the excessive inventory on hand with respect to slow-moving stock. (2) It increases the amount of available working capital the business owner may require to meet specific commitments or to restock inventory with new merchandise. (3) It attracts new customers to the store who may have come as bargain hunters but who may become regular customers at some other time. Generally, then, sales promotions are effective action steps. However, sales promotions held at random when all merchandise is reduced without purpose or planning tend to create the image of a bargain operation, unless you plan to operate this type of business.

Referrals from satisfied customers. Many business owners believe that only service-oriented businesses rely on referrals in marketing their business. It is true that service and professional businesses acquire most of their customers through referrals, but they are also an essential marketing tool for all types of businesses. The procedure is simple. If customers believe that they have been fairly treated, they will tell others. Conversely, referrals can work against you. A discrediting referral from a customer or client can be many times more damaging than one good referral. In some cases, referrals come about naturally, but it may often become necessary for a business owner to request referrals from regular customers. There is nothing improper in such a request if it is done in a businesslike manner. The owner simply asks the customer to keep the business in mind if they know other people who could use the products or services. In this case, human nature can act in favor of the business owner because people take pride in being asked to recommend businesses that have established good reputations.

Market-sensitive pricing. One of the most sensitive factors in marketing is the question of pricing. Determining the price of goods and services can be confusing to some business operators. For example, many owners price according to what the market will bear. In many situations, this method of pricing may offer the only alternative. Although some new owners may cut the prices of their products in order to take customers away from their competitors, it is not recommended. Usually it only brings those customers who are bargain hunting and who will eventually drift on to the next bargain. There is no loyalty with this type of customer. However, maintaining a price at the same level as the competition or a little below competitive prices is the best policy to follow for the new owner.

Another aspect of pricing relates to the type of product for sale. For example, in pricing jewelry, paintings and arts and crafts, which sometimes have more aesthetic than material value, the price the buyer will pay is determined by the subjective value placed on the article. Value or price is in the eyes of the beholder. This does not mean that the seller can demand any price, but it does mean that the price is greatly influenced by the customer's perceptions of an object's intrinsic worth.

Certain basic products and services fall into the area of necessities, such as food, gasoline, medicine, clothes, legal and accounting services, and so forth. The price determination for these products and services is indicated by the market itself and by the prices established by competitive forces. Thus, it is fairly easy to establish prices on items that have definite basic or intrinsic worth. A problem arises when an item has both basic and aesthetic characteristics. An example of this is today's automobile, which must be desirable in the eyes of the consumer as well as have basic performance characteristics. The automobile industry overcomes the problem through diversification, namely by manufacturing a basic car for the consumer expecting economical performance and a more luxurious car for the consumer desiring a car with distinctive lines, beauty, and comfort regardless of performance. As a small business owner, you will not be able to satisfy the public with such diverse variations of the same product; the cost would not justify the action. A less costly and flexible approach to pricing your product is needed in order to establish a composite price to reflect both the basic market value and the consumer's perceived requirements.

Personalized services is yet another area of marketing many business owners fail to recognize as a merchandising tool, whereas big businesses are often unable to relate on a personal basis to various customers' needs. Customers become a number in a computer, which often offends the customer by taking away the personal touch. So, as a business owner of a smaller operation, you can capitalize on this particular short-coming of big business by establishing a merchandising policy based on the personal needs of customers. An example of how personalized service can be an essential merchandising tool is shown by the actions of some of the larger discount operations. When these stores first opened, it was their primary objective to offer only enough service to quickly turn inventory. But as competition among the big discounters increased, many of these chains established information centers to answer customer inquiries and to assist the customer with his particular shopping needs. The lumber departments of the Channel and Rickel chains are good examples of information centers available, in this case, to do-it-yourselfers.

Advertising is generally recognized as a major marketing factor. Unfortunately, there is no general rule that business owners can follow regarding the amount of funds to set aside for advertising. The problem business owners must resolve is how to measure the effectiveness of advertising per dollar expended.

Advertising is a merchandising tool intended to bring the business owner's product or service to the attention of the public. With today's news media and rapid network of communication available around the world, advertising has become a giant enterprise. For the small business owner, the cost of advertising must be carefully measured to ensure that the advertising program is having a positive effect on increasing sales. Most business owners utilize direct advertising with greater success than institutional advertising. Direct advertising places the product directly in the limelight, whereas institutional advertising keeps the owner's trade name before the public.

One of the most sensible ways for the average business owner to measure the effect of advertising and to determine the market being penetrated by the advertising is to try the following procedure: (1) place an advertisement in a local newspaper announcing a drawing to be held at your store, which requires the customer to bring in the advertisement in order to enter the contest; (2) when customers come to the store with the advertisement, have them complete a card showing their name and address; (3) a prize should be awarded that is newsworthy enough to be placed in the local papers.

The advantages of such techniques are numerous. They can quickly demonstrate the effectiveness of an advertising program as well as define the market being penetrated. Additionally, they can supply a mailing list, some free publicity, and some new customers who have entered your store for the first time.

The successful business owner utilizes many advertising tools in order to make his marketing program more effective. In the last analysis, advertising cannot be allocated as a percentage of sales; it must be a specific program with the specific goal of bringing your product or service to the attention of the consumer.

Quite often business people fail to effectively follow through on the results of their service or use of their product. When this is allowed to happen, they are failing to test the marketability of their product or service. A follow-through procedure is another marketing tool and can often be accomplished by asking the public to fill out a simple questionnaire rating your product against others. On a smaller scale, a telephone call to a customer after a service has been performed is also a legitimate follow-through technique. Whatever method is used, it is essential to ascertain if your product or service is compatible with that of the competition in both acceptability and price. A comprehensive follow-through program is one highly effective way of doing it.

Diversification. A merchandising sales program would not be complete without consideration of diversification of products or services to widen your merchandise base. The primary purpose of diversification is to promote expansion and growth in your business; you must also keep in mind that without diversification the business may become flat or stale. Businesses that fail to take advantage of new customer items or that fail to discern the changing desires of customers may find themselves out of step with market reality in a short period of time. The "in thing" is whatever sells. What is "in" today can be "out" tomorrow. Thus, marketing programs must remain flexible enough to meet the changing desires of the consumer. Furthermore, overespecialization that restricts the business operator to one or two products can constrict the

overall marketing program by stifling any opportunity for
further growth.*

Without this type of marketing program, what would the
ABC Company have done the next time it experienced a sales
decline? It is true that the ABC Company had a sales projection based upon a continual rapport with their customers,
but the program lacked an aggressive approach and at best
seemed rather complacent to the point of being routine. For
example, it lacked any approach to product diversification.
In short, what new products did ABC have to offer? None.
What about modification of their present product line? Had
they initiated a product modification program, it would not
have been necessary for one of their customers to request a
redesign effort on an existing product. It was the quick
thinking to step up their in-house efforts with the Smith
Company, modifying the component part that eventually
turned the second quarter around and resulted in greater
sales volume. But the action should not have been initiated
out of sheer desperation. It should have already been an essential part of their existing marketing program. *The rule to
remember is that you cannot sustain your cash projections
in sales without the support of a well-balanced and implemented marketing program.*

Inventory Control

Under an effective inventory control system there would
have been no increase in the level of inventory during the
first quarter. In the case of the ABC Company, where inventory levels were increasing each month, immediate action
based on a perpetual inventory control system could have

*Excerpted, with permission, from Emery Toncré, *The Action-Step Plan to Owning
and Operating a Successful Business* (Englewood Cliffs, N.J.: Prentice-Hall, 1983),
pp. 30–34.

been initiated and reversed the trend. Under a perpetual inventory control system, inventory levels are constantly adjusted to reflect sales and purchases of resale material. Furthermore, inventory being maintained on a perpetual basis reflects decreases from sales and increases from purchases, item by item. As a matter of record, the action finally taken by ABC in the second quarter would have been unnecessary under a perpetual inventory control system. Such action as discounting obsolete inventory at reduced prices is not a step normally taken by a business that has an inventory control system in place. An effective system highlights obsolete items automatically, establishing acceptable inventory levels on a perpetual basis. Thus, ABC Company had a surplus of obsolete inventory on hand to sell because the purchase of resale items was not carefully reviewed in terms of potential sales before they were purchased. An inventory control program is a must if you expect your cash management program to be successful.

Expense Controls

When sales volume dropped and ABC adjusted its projected expense to lower levels of sales activity, no one was quite sure at the time if the lower expense projections would compensate for the drop in sales volume by still providing an acceptable profit margin. Furthermore, there was no guarantee that ABC would be able to hold the actual expenses to these levels. This was obvious from the first quarter results. In fact, ABC's actions were the exact reverse of what is considered a constructive approach to expense controls. For ABC to accept a drop in sales volume without knowing the effect on profits by first determining the effect on expenses is totally unacceptable. A more suitable approach for ABC would have been to determine if the actual expense could be realistically trimmed to meet the reduced sales level before arbitrarily reducing the sales projection. If this action step was deemed impossible, the reduction in sales volume should never have been approved (see Exhibit 5-23).

In Exhibit 5-23, you will note on first glance that the drop in sales volume from $100,000 to $80,000 would still generate a profit of $5,000. However, when you take into consideration that the actual variable expenses are anticipated to be $30,000 instead of $25,000 (a $5,000 increase over projection), a drop in sales volume from $100,000 to $80,000 would generate a loss of $10,000. In retrospect, it is now apparent that ABC was lucky its actual expenses held to projected levels, which is not always the case. Thus, the recovery in the second quarter was accomplished by capping all expense items. You will note that this was done by stopping payment on most expense items. Although this action proved to be effective in the short run for the second quarter, it can only be considered a stopgap measure.

A bona fide expense control system begins before the expense is committed. For example, let's examine the payroll expense item more carefully. If you will recall, sales volume for the ABC Company was dropping drastically during the first quarter while the existing payroll remained virtually unchanged. What is the real problem behind this apparent lack of expense control with employee payroll? *ABC lacked the management tools of an employee program to make immediate reductions in payroll beyond the point of simple termination of a few workers.* Prior to the second quarter ABC requested that the individual supervisors review the workers' performance. As you recall they found duplication in the work being performed, incompetency, low productivity, and an overall feeling of complacency on the part of the work force. The implementation of a sound and effective employee program would have corrected these problems long before ABC happened to stumble upon them in desperation.

Let's examine the expenses of advertising, travel, and entertainment more closely. It was decided in the second quarter that these items would have to be increased in order

EXHIBIT 5-23. Expense Control Analysis for ABC Company

	Initial Projection	Adjusted Projections	
		For Sales Volume	For Sales Volume and Expenses
Sales	$100,000	$80,000	$ 80,000
Cost of Sales	50,000	50,000	50,000
Gross Profit	$ 50,000	$30,000	$ 30,000
Expenses			
Fixed	10,000	10,000	10,000
Projected Variable	30,000	25,000	30,000 } Anticipated Variable
Total Expenses	$ 40,000	$35,000	$ 40,000
Profit or Loss	$ 10,000	$ 5,000	$(10,000)
Profit or Loss Percentage to Sales	10%	6%	0%

to support additional efforts in sales. The question that was never answered by the ABC Company was how much increase should be allowed and under whose authority. In short, in order to sustain an effective expense control within the guidelines of your cash management program, specific rules must be adopted and practiced in order to support your efforts:

1. Each expense item must be identified down to the source of its increase or decrease.

2. Responsibility for committing to a specific expense must be placed at the lowest level within the organization.

3. Expenses must be reviewed on the basis of their total performance. This allows some expenses to exceed projected targets, offsetting other expense items that fall below anticipated projections.

4. Expenses allowed to increase over projected levels must be correlated to meet the projected limits of future sales activity. For example, advertising must simply not be allowed to increase to any amount. The additional increase must be offset by increased sales activities for the months ahead. If not, the purpose of allowing the item to increase over projection has been defeated.

Balance Sheet Control

In spite of what may have appeared to have happened to the ABC Company's balance sheet in the second quarter, in reality ABC made no lasting effort to change the results or place constructive controls over specific items that affected the level of working capital. If you recall, cash-on-hand increased because inventory levels were curtailed. This was accomplished through an inventory control action rather than a balance sheet effort. In short, the ABC Company had no formal balance sheet control program to reinforce the cash management program. *The purpose of a balance sheet control is to ensure that the projected levels of working capital reflected in the cash management program are achieved.*

Let's examine some of the various balance sheet items where long-term controls should have been implemented. Accounts receivable must be supported by a listing of customers that shows the name, address, amount, and date of each invoice. This report is called an aging of the accounts receivable because it determines the time span between the initial due date of the invoice and the date of the present outstanding balance. As a rule, most customers pay within 30 to 60 days. If the account exceeds 120 days, most business owners consider some type of action for collection.

Collecting overdue accounts receivable has become more difficult over the last several years because of tight monetary policies within the business community. Collection agencies now have so many requests for help that many of them concentrate on only the higher outstanding amounts and those businesses most likely to pay. Some business owners have threatened to take customers to court while others have obtained legal action on past due invoices. No one system seems to be more effective than another, so business owners must rely on their judgment to decide what action would be best to take with delinquent customers. There are some lessons to remember in this area. Whatever action you decide to take, follow it through until the matter is resolved. If you delay action or take no action at all, you may find that your customer in the interim has gone bankrupt or closed her doors, leaving you with nothing but a past due invoice.

The acquisition of a tangible asset should always be reviewed in respect to its cash effect on your balance sheet. An evaluation study that supports the need for an asset does not automatically imply that you can afford the acquisition or that it should be purchased regardless of your present cash position.

Accounts payable is similar to accounts receivable, except

you may now be the delinquent customer. Control over balance sheet items, like all items, is only effective if handled at the point of commitment.

It should be apparent to you at this point that each balance sheet item requires separate attention. Control, however, requires a careful assessment. *The object of the balance sheet control program is to ensure a substantial level of cash-on-hand in accordance with your cash management program.* This point is illustrated in more detail in Exhibit 5-24. In this exhibit, cash dropped from a projected $10,000 to a $5,000 level. In reviewing the financial conditions, one should note the fact that some balance sheet items cannot be changed easily; in this case, such items as payment of taxes, payment of bank loan, cost of capital stock, and prior retained earnings will have to be considered partially fixed in our efforts to regain a sufficient working capital. Therefore, we are left with accounts receivable, accounts payable, inventory levels, and equipment acquisitions as possible areas where effective changes can be made more readily within the guidelines of a constructive balance sheet control program.

In controlling balance sheet items one must remember the following points:

1. Sustaining a sufficient working cash level is the objective.

2. Each balance sheet item must be treated separately with respect to changes and the effect of these changes must be interrelated into a total financial picture affecting the balance sheet as a whole. For example, an all-out effort to reduce accounts receivable to gain additional cash for the purchase of a useless piece of equipment would certainly not be considered a constructive action.

3. Controlling your balance sheet in a proper manner that ensures sufficient levels of working capital will be re-

EXHIBIT 5-24. ABC Company Balance Sheet Control

	Projected	Actual	Action Steps
Assets			
Cash	$ 10,000	$ 5,000	End Result
Accounts Receivable	25,000	40,000	Customer Control
Inventory	50,000	50,000	Inventory Control
Equipment (Net Depreciation)	56,000	56,000	Acquisition of Equipment Control
Other Assets	5,000	5,000	Constant
Total	$146,000	$156,000	
Liabilities			
Accounts Payable	30,000	40,000	Accounts Payable Control
Tax Payable	5,000	5,000	Profit and Loss Control
Bank Loans	80,000	80,000	Constant
Total	$115,000	$125,000	
Net Worth			
Capital Stock	1,000	1,000	Constant
Retained Earnings	20,000	20,000	Profit and Loss Control
Profit for the Period	10,000	10,000	Profit and Loss Control
Total	$ 31,000	$ 31,000	
Total Liabilities and Net Worth	$146,000	$156,000	

143

flected in your cash management program by higher sustained levels of cash.

Cash is the needed catalyst to push through effective business actions. Cash is needed to take advantage of an opportunity. Finally, cash is needed to stay in business. In short, cash represents the bottom line that governs all business decisions and activities.

6

AUTOMATION

Small business owners who desire to automate their cash management programs must first consider many factors. In this chapter I will deal with some of the problems of automation, such as the present relationship between the small business operator and the evolution of the computer, how to decide when the move to automation is justified, the essential factors for the automation of a cash control program, and finally the advantages to be gained through automation by the ABC Company.

When computers made their debut into the small business community, the average business owner was taken by total surprise. In the beginning two problems existed: (1) the business owner did not understand the computer, and (2) the essential software needed to resolve troublesome business problems was lacking. There were many factors that contributed to this misunderstanding. To begin with, many small business owners not only lacked an understanding of what computers could do but assumed the computer was the answer to all their problems. Some thought computers were like television sets and could simply be plugged into the wall to get results. For those businesses who sold computers to the small business owners, the focus of attention was on selling equipment to be used for eventual automation, not on the day-to-day problems affecting the business owner's operations.

With the help of mass advertising that encouraged business owners to buy their very own computers to resolve their problems, the computer market finally became saturated, with thousands of useless computers sitting on business owners' desks. For many small business owners, the promises of profits through automation have given way to the acceptance of the computer as a mere *paperweight*. Let me illustrate my point with two case histories.

In the first example, I assisted a client who had a serious problem in collecting her outstanding accounts receivables. In my opinion her problem was due to many factors, including the way her customers were billed, the need to request prepayment prior to completing her work, a nonexistent credit check prior to accepting a new customer, and a total lack of follow-up on overdue customers. Her approach to the problem was the acquisition of a computer that would detail existing accounts receivable customers. Without any consideration of the cost of the computer, not to mention the cost of the operator's time, my client purchased a computer and the corresponding software program necessary for automating the accounts receivable. After considerable cost in time and money, she finally acquired an accounts receivable program that detailed customers by name, invoice date, and amount due. What she did not receive was a better collection approach.

In a similar case a client was hoping to replace his two bookkeepers with an automated bookkeeping program. He managed to terminate the two employees easily but was never able to automate the new bookkeeping system. What happened? Was there a problem with the computer? The answer is no, because a computer does exactly what it is programmed to do. The problem was with the small business owner who did not understand the capability of his new acquisition. The gap between the computer's capability and the problems that the business owner needs to resolve is slowly being closed by a new group of professional systems specialists whose prime purpose is to fit your needs as business owners to the capabilities of your personal computer. Although it now appears that the gap has been narrowed at least for the moment, confusion still prevails. Systems specialists who have the knowledge to resolve your business needs through automation are in great demand and therefore are difficult to find. Consequently, the larger businesses within the small business community are the first group who can afford the high professional fees of these qualified people. This still leaves the smaller business owners with the same unanswered questions regarding their computer. Another area which still confuses the average business owner is buying software programs from shelf stock and still finding himself unable to gain an overall resolution to their business problems. Shelf software is designed to provide you with specific answers for specific problems. For example, one can easily find programs for automating accounts receivable, accounts payable, balance sheet preparation, bookkeeping control and payroll records. The software program that the business owner needs most, but is not likely to find easily, is an overall program that links all the various shelf programs together into one common program specifically designed to meet their own particular needs.

JUSTIFICATION FOR ACQUIRING A COMPUTER

For many years large corporations have practiced a procedure of justifying the need for the computer before acquisition. During the early stages of computer growth the cost of establishing an automated computer system was expensive enough to warrant thorough cost assessments prior to acquisition. Today, the cost of computers for small businesses has been so drastically reduced that many consider the need to justify such a purchase academic. As a result, justification procedures, always considered an absolute must for large corporations, have never been considered necessary by small businesses. I believe that a justification procedure should be adopted by all businesses, irrespective of cost, to ensure the business owner that the right decision is being made. Let's examine some factors essential to justifying the acquisition of the computer.

Cost Versus Savings

There are pluses and minuses that govern the acquisition of a computer. If the acquisition of the computer is for the prime purpose of automation and cannot save more than it costs, what's the purpose of the acquisition? Therefore, before acquiring a computer the business owner should carefully compare the cost to the potential savings. The cost of automation includes the cost not only of the computer but also of software programs, operating employees, supplies, maintenance and repairs, and some allowance for additional growth through the acquisition of additional equipment. Savings from automation include the savings of clerical employees, greater productivity, speed of reporting, greater accuracy, and mass reporting of information at one time. Unfortunately, some savings are intangible and cannot be accurately measured. For example, if you can take corrective action more quickly as the result of automation and therefore generate additional profits, the estimated savings can be used to further justify your action to automate.

Equipment Selection

The small business computer market is no longer dominated by one or two major suppliers. Today there are many suppliers competing in a tight competitive market. Computer manufacturers are constantly improving their hardware capabilities in order to gain an advantage over their competitors. With such a diversity of computers on the market, the problem of selecting the computer that will best serve your needs is a difficult one. Nevertheless, all factors pertaining to the equipment must be carefully considered, including dependability of the equipment, service policy in case of breakdowns, price compared to compatible equipment, delivery and installation cost, and finally design allowances for advances in technology as your needs in business expand with the growth of your operations. Many of these assessments are not easily made and professional assistance in the computer field may be necessary. It is important to remember the price alone is not the only deciding factor to consider before your final acquisition.

Additional Technical Support

I have often witnessed small business owners shackled with computers that were totally ineffective, with nowhere to turn for help. Nothing can be more frustrating to business owners than to purchase a computer in good faith with promises of technical support and reassurances by the supplier that the computer will perform specific tasks and then find themselves at the mercy of high-priced systems specialists to select or write the software programs required to make the computer work in concert with their operations. The only practical action you can take as a small business owner to avoid this problem is to start with the premise that you know nothing about computers and fully expect to be instructed until you understand the basic requirements needed to make your computer an integral part of your operation. Therefore, your acquisition should be contractually supported by all the technical assistance you may require.

ESSENTIAL FACTORS FOR AUTOMATION

Let's now turn our attention to the automation of the cash management program.* In general, there are many software packages available for automating cash. Many of these pro-

---

*An automated system that meets the requirements of the cash management program described in this text has been designed by Emery Toncré & Associates, 7 Fox Chase Lane, Convent Station, NJ, 07961.

grams are flexible enough to be utilized on a variety of personal computers. However, there are some notable exceptions. First, some software packages are specifically tailored to more powerful computers than the general personal computer. And although software programs of all types are plentiful, system specialists are not always available to assist the smaller business operator.

Let's review the essential criteria required to automate a cash management program. First, the program must offer more than a simple reporting system of information. Knowing the financial facts more quickly than before is a plus factor, but being able to compare this information to established objectives is another step forward. There are many software programs designed to report cash results, but only a few that make comparisons to the business projections. Second, the initial projections with the cash management program require a software package that automatically readjusts the initial projections to actual results, reflecting those changes to the initial projection that would be unacceptable as profitable objectives. This provides business owners with the opportunity to determine if they should change their initial objectives to reflect current results and establish new projections for their businesses. Third, a well-balanced cash management program should encompass the effect of all supportive programs, such as inventory control, as part of its total software package. The cash management program does not need just a program for reporting financial results, but a software package that combines financial projections with supporting programs. Finally, a program of this magnitude requires that the software package be developed in two stages. The first stage automates the basic factors within the program that are common to all businesses. The second stage adjusts the basic software package to meet the individual needs of a particular business. Many business owners have used the first-stage software to test their abilities to operate a prototype model of an average small business operation.

ADVANTAGES THROUGH AUTOMATION

Automation of its cash management program would provide the ABC Company with essential information more quickly for management action. The faster corrective action can be taken, the greater the savings of cash profits. Under the clerical method of implementing a cash management program, the ABC Company did not know how bad the first quarter results were until the beginning of the second quarter. By this time ABC was almost on the brink of failure. If ABC had had an automated cash management program, the results would have been available for review on a monthly basis (see Exhibits 6-1 through 6-6). To have produced this same amount of information clerically within the same time span would have been an impossible undertaking. Having this information on a monthly basis would have enabled ABC to take action at the end of each month. For example, let's review the monthly results for January (see Exhibits 6-1 and 6-2).

The warning signals indicated problems in the first month with accounts receivable and ending inventory. Let's assume that the ABC Company initiated action regarding these two warning signals in January. In Exhibit 6-1, ABC Company Balance Sheet for January, called for a reduction in accounts receivables of $10,000, reducing the opening balance of $30,000 to $20,000. Actual reduction from the opening accounts receivables was only $5,000 ($30,000 less $25,000). A computer list was made for January of past due accounts, who were immediately contacted about the current balance in their accounts. The results of this quick action by ABC increased cash collections by $5,000 in both February and March (see Exhibits 6-1 and 6-3), which reflected an increase in inventory for both January and February. From a perpetual inventory control system a list of inventory items was immediately prepared for review. ABC then took steps to reduce purchases and initiate a sales promotion program to sell off obsolete inventory at discounted prices. The results

EXHIBIT 6-1. ABC Company Balance Sheet January (monthly projection compared to actual)

	Opening Balance Sheet January 1	January Balance Sheet Projected	January Balance Sheet Actual
Assets			
Cash on Hand	$ -0-	$ 5,733	$ (15,117)
Accounts Receivable	30,000	20,000	25,000[a]
Inventory on Hand	20,000	50,000	70,000[b]
Equipment	125,000	140,000	140,000
Less Depreciation	-0-	5,000	5,000
	125,000	135,000	135,000
Total Assets	175,000	210,733	214,883
Liabilities and Net Worth			
Accounts Payable	40,000	65,000	65,000
Bank Loan	80,000	78,333	78,333
Total Liabilities	120,000	143,333	143,333
Net Worth			
Capital Stock	1,000	1,000	1,000
Shareholders' Investment	40,000	45,100	42,000
Retained Earnings	14,000	21,300	28,550
Total Net Worth	55,000	67,400	71,550
Total Liabilities and Net Worth	$175,000	$210,733	$214,883

Warning signals affecting cash funds:

[a]Accounts receivable actually decreased compared to the opening balance sheet January 1 by $5,000 ($30,000 opening balance less $25,000 actual balance), projected decrease in accounts receivable called for a reduction of $10,000 ($30,000 less $20,000) loss to cash: $5,000 compared to projection.

[b]Ending inventory actually increased by $50,000 from the opening balance sheet January 1 ($20,000 opening balance to $70,000 actual balance), projected increase in inventory called for an increase of only $30,000 ($20,000 to $50,000), cash gain: $20,000 compared to projection. The action, however, resulted in greater levels of inventory compared to projection.

EXHIBIT 6-2. ABC Company Cash Flow Analysis January (monthly projection compared to actual)

	Cash Flow Comparison Opening Balance Sheet to Projected Balance Sheet Ending January	Cash Flow Comparison Opening Balance Sheet to Actual Balance Sheet Ending January
Cash Sources		
Net Income (from Profit & Loss)	$ 7,300	$ 14,550
Other Sources of Cash		
Depreciation	$ 5,000	$ 5,000
Accounts Payable Income	25,000	25,000
Shareholders' Investment	5,100	2,000
Accounts Receivable Decrease	10,000	5,000
	45,000	37,000
Total	52,400	51,550
Application of Cash Funds		
Equipment Purchases	15,000	15,000
Inventory Increase	30,000	30,000
Bank Loan Payment	1,667	1,667
Total Application of Funds	46,667	66,677
Cash on Hand Increase or (Decrease)	$ 5,733	$(15,117)

153

EXHIBIT 6-3. ABC Company Balance Sheet February (monthly projection compared to actual)

	Balance Sheet Ending January		February Balance Sheet			
			Projected		Actual	
Assets						
Cash on Hand		$ (15,117)		$ 10,516		$ (13,284)
Accounts Receivable		25,000		30,000		20,000
Inventory on Hand		70,000		50,000		110,000[a]
Equipment	140,000		140,000		140,000	
Less Depreciation	5,000	135,000	10,000	130,000	10,000	130,000
Total Assets		214,883		220,516		246,716
Liabilities and Net Worth						
Accounts Payable		65,000		65,000		70,000[b]
Bank Loan		78,333		76,666		76,666
Total Liabilities		143,333		141,666		145,666
Net Worth						
Capital Stock		1,000		1,000		1,000
Shareholders' Investment		42,000		42,000		70,000[c]
Retained Earnings		28,550		35,850		20,050
Total Net Worth		71,550		78,850		100,050
Total Liabilities and Net Worth		$214,883		$220,516		$246,716

Warning signals affecting cash funds:

[a]Ending inventory actually increased by $40,000 ($70,000 opening balance to $110,000 actual balance), the projection called for a decrease in inventory of only $20,000 ($70,000 to $50,000); the action, however, resulted in greater levels of inventory compared to projection.

[b]Accounts payable actually increased by $5,000 ($65,000 opening balance to $70,000 actual balance), resulting in holding invoices due vendors. The projection called for no change.

[c]Shareholders required to make an additional investment of $28,000 ($42,000 opening balance to $70,000 actual balance); actually cash gain: $28,000. The projection called for no change.

EXHIBIT 6-4. ABC Company Cash Flow Analysis February (monthly projection compared to actual)

	Cash Flow Comparison Opening Balance Sheet to Projected Balance Sheet Ending February		Cash Flow Comparison Opening Balance Sheet to Actual Balance Sheet Ending February	
Cash Sources				
Net Income		$ 7,300		$ 550
Other Sources of Cash				
Depreciation	$ 5,000		$ 5,000	
Accounts Payable Increase	–0–		5,000	
Shareholders' Investment	–0–		28,000	
Inventory Decrease	20,000		–0–	
Accounts Receivable Decrease	–0–	25,000	5,000	43,500
Total Cash Source		32,300		43,500
Application of Cash Funds				
Accounts Receivable Increase	5,000		–0–	
Bank Loan Payment	1,667		1,667	
Inventory Increase	–0–		40,000	
Total Application of Funds		6,667		41,667
Cash on Hand Increase or (Decrease)		$ 25,633		$ 1,833
Cash, Balance February 1		(15,117)		(15,117)
Cash on Hand		$ 10,516		$(13,284)

155

EXHIBIT 6-5. ABC Company Balance Sheet March (monthly projection compared to actual)

	Balance Sheet Ending February	March Balance Sheet Projected	March Balance Sheet Actual
Assets			
Cash on Hand	$ (13,284)	$ 10,000	$ 2,000
Accounts Receivable	20,000	35,000	15,000
Inventory on Hand	110,000	50,000	100,000"
Equipment	140,000		140,000
Less Depreciation	10,000		15,000
	130,000	125,000	125,000
Total Assets	246,716	220,000	242,000
Liabilities and Net Worth			
Accounts Payable	70,000	63,000	77,720"
Bank Loan	76,666	75,000	75,000
Total Liabilities	146,666	138,000	152,720
Net Worth			
Capital Stock	1,000	1,000	1,000
Shareholders' Investment	70,000	45,100	90,000'
		(450)	(2,670)
Retained Earnings	29,050	36,350	950
Total Net Worth	100,050	82,000	89,280
Total Liabilities and Net Worth	$246,716	$220,000	$242,000

Warning signals affecting cash funds:

"Inventory on hand actually decreased by $10,000 but still remains far in excess of projected level of $50,000 ($110,000 opening balance to $100,000 actual balance).

"Accounts payable actually increased by $7,720 ($70,000 opening balance to $77,720 actual balance). Accounts payable was projected to decrease by $7,000 ($70,000 opening balance to $63,000 projected balance). Actual cash gain of $7,720 was achieved by holding vendors' invoices.

'Shareholders required to invest an additional $20,000 ($70,000 opening balance to $90,000 actual balance). Actual cash gain $20,000. Total additional investment within the 3-month period compared to the initial projection of $44,900 ($45,100 projection to $90,000 actual)

EXHIBIT 6-6. **ABC Company Cash Flow Analysis March (monthly projection compared to actual)**

	Cash Flow Comparison Balance Sheet Ending February to Projected Balance Sheet Ending March	Cash Flow Comparison Balance Sheet Ending February to Actual Balance Sheet Ending March
Cash Sources		
Net Income	$ 7,300	$(28,100)
Tax Adjustment	(450)	(2,670)
Other Sources of Cash		
Inventory Decrease	60,000	10,000
Depreciation	$ 5,000	$ 5,000
Accounts Payable Increase	–0–	7,720
Shareholders' Investment	–0–	20,000
Accounts Receivable Decrease	–0–	5,000
	65,000	47,720
Total Cash Source	71,850	16,950
Application of Cash Funds		
Accounts Receivable Increase	15,000	
Bank Loan Payment	1,666	
Shareholders' Investment	24,900	1,666
Accounts Payable Decrease	7,000	
Total Application of Funds	48,566	1,666
Cash on Hand Increase or (Decrease)	$ 23,284	$ 15,284
Cash Balance March 1	(13,284)	(13,284)
Cash on Hand	$ 10,000	$ 2,000

157

of this effort reduced inventory by $10,000 by the end of March. In both examples, ABC Company was able to move quickly and decisively utilizing the computer. Let's now turn our attention to Exhibit 6-5, to see the effect on cash resulting from ABC's effort. Exhibits 6-1 and 6-6 show that ABC's cash on hand after computer automation increased from a $15,117 loss in January to a $2,000 balance in March.

For the ABC Company, then, the combination of quick action based on fast results through automation proved to be profitable.

Automation with the personal computer can be a very useful management tool for the small business owner. But remember there are rules to follow: *(1) develop a plan for utilizing your computer before acquisition; (2) justify your acquisition by assessing your basic needs; (3) select the proper software package to achieve the objectives of your cash management program; and (4) make sure that your computer is utilized as a constructive management tool in concert with your basic business decisions and cash management program.*

7

CASH, THE EQUALIZER

If conducting one's business in a successful manner is a game of economic survival in which the ultimate winner is the player who seizes upon every opportunity to gain the advantage, then cash must be considered its final equalizer. I cannot conceive of any action on the part of a business owner that does not result in either favorable or unfavorable consequences. Furthermore, I would be hard pressed to identify any action initiated by a business owner that was not based on cash considerations. In the first section of the text, I described in considerable detail the steps necessary to develop a cash management program, starting with the fundamentals and the need for cash controls and then moving to the factors essential to implement a well-balanced and totally comprehensive program. By this time, I am sure there is little doubt in your mind that cash funds must be controlled in order for your business to become successful and continue to stay profitable. But if you are like most business owners, you will find some excuse to delay the implementation of cash control efforts, allowing them to drift into a secondary position well behind other business problems you judge to be more pressing. Over the years, I have found this practice to be the rule 90 percent of the time. Although I have no way of proving my contention, I simply believe that most business owners find the subject of cash control far too complex to comprehend. Furthermore, many business owners underestimate the amount of influence available cash funds have on their day-to-day business decisions. In this chapter, I am going to endeavor to dispense with the misconception that cash is no more than just a dollar amount in the business owner's checkbook.

I am going to relate a story. It's not a pretty story, but it's a true case history with such twists and turns that even three years later, I still find the events that occurred both bizarre and baffling, sometimes ridiculous, almost always without justification, and often very sad. As this case history begins to unfold, it is my contention that you will become a believer in cash controls. You will see how the lack and even the surplus of available cash funds became the underlying factor that governs every greedy decision made by the principals in this case history. In the end, the actions of the principals became vicious, with cash becoming the equalizer that determined the unwarranted actions of each principal to reach his objective.

When our firm was introduced to the XYZ Company, it was on the verge of bankruptcy. Our client, the bank, was one of the major creditors of the XYZ Company, with an outstanding loan of $600,000. We were assigned the task of assessing the existing conditions within the company to determine if the operation could be reconstituted into a profitable business.

If we recommended a rebuilding program, it would then be our task to implement this effort and ensure that our work resulted in a profitable conclusion. We accepted the work on the condition that our client would pay the professional fees on a monthly basis, with the provision that if we were unsuccessful in rebuilding the XYZ Company our total fee would be discounted by 15 percent. To us the assignment was a challenge. For the bank it represented an action of last resort to recover their initial losses. For the principals of the XYZ Company, however, the consulting assignment was a farce because they had already given up the possibility of recovery six months prior to our introduction to the company.

In order to understand the events that led up to its present state of affairs better, let me first describe XYZ Company's early development.

The XYZ Company was bought in 1977 by three principals, John as president, Tom as treasurer and secretary, and Bob as vice president of operations. Prior to acquisition the company had researched and developed two major machine parts essential to the defense industry. Over the past 15 years of operation, the government contracts had grown to represent about 60 percent of its total sales volume. The previous owners enjoyed a profitable operation over the years, with the usual ups and downs that all small- to medium-size businesses experience.

In 1977, one of the original founders of the company passed away and the remaining shareholders decided to sell the company. The company was then acquired from its previous owners for the total sum of $900,000, $600,000 from a collateralized bank loan and $300,000 equally invested by each of the three principals. The business had been handled well and represented an attractive buy to anyone searching for an established and profitable operation. For the three principals who acquired the company, it was the opportunity they had been waiting for. As a result, the closing went very smoothly, with very few questions being raised and all parties satisfied with the final acquisition.

On February 25, 1977, the company was acquired by John, Tom, and Bob and renamed the XYZ Company. The corporate charter was revised, and the responsibilities and duties of the three principals were placed in the minutes of the first corporate meeting of the shareholders. John was elected president, with full responsibility to develop and direct all marketing and sales efforts. Tom was elected treasurer and secretary, with total responsibility for all financial matters, and Bob was elected vice president of operations. Each one willingly pledged his personal assets to the bank to back the initial $600,000 loan. The transition of ownership proceeded very smoothly. The existing customers, including the various people in governmental agencies directly involved in defense orders, were advised of the ownership change. Two key people from the former company stayed on with the XYZ Company in a consulting capacity to ensure stability within the company during the transition. The employees were carefully reassured that no changes were contemplated in the immediate future that would affect their present job status. Vendors were contacted and informed of the change in ownership. Credit references were supplied to all vendors requesting a financial update by the bank. Outside professional assistance was retained by the same law firm that was instrumental in the acquisition and final closing. An accounting firm was recommended by the law firm and retained for financial statements and related tax requirements. The transition proceeded so smoothly that everyone failed to notice that the transition steps were actually being completed by the two key people from the previous company retained to assist the XYZ Company, while the three principals John, Tom, and Bob stood by as casual observers. Unknown to anyone was the ominous fact that neither John nor Tom had any knowledge of or experience in operating a small business, and that Bob's experience was limited to operations, leaving them no choice but to allow the previous personnel to continue to operate the company. To make matters worse, all three individuals were convinced that operating the XYZ Company was simple and that they could learn all that was necessary as the business continued to progress. Adding further to the confusion was the assumption that each individual believed the other principal had more than enough experience to overcome any small business problems and eventually make their acquisition a profitable investment.

To gain a better understanding of how poorly prepared this consortium of new owners was for operating a small business, let me describe the background of each, their personal characteristics, and how each of them prepared himself before stepping into the business world of entrepreneurs.

John, who became president, was the oldest of the three principals. After college he started his corporate climb with primary emphasis in marketing and sales. His last position prior to the acquisition was vice president of sales and marketing development. Of the three principals, it was John who first became aware that the soon to be renamed XYZ Company was for sale. He became aware of the potential acquisition strictly by accident, due to the fact that his company sold component parts to the XYZ Company before it was offered for sale. Thus it was through John's efforts that the XYZ Company was identified as a possible acquisition, and it was his carefully orchestrated salesmanship that convinced Tom and Bob to join him in this venture. As a result, it was only natural that both Tom and Bob looked to him for leadership. Whether John qualified as the leader of the group was unfortunately never questioned, at least not in the beginning. By nature John was a born risk-taker. His ability as a polished salesperson also made him vulnerable to other talented salespeople. In short, given the opportunity, he could sell almost anything, but he could also be sold on a product or idea quite easily.

Consequently, he never evaluated his actions prior to the acquisition of XYZ Company. Fortunately for him and his two associates, the XYZ Company was a solid company with good growth potential. However, he never asked the one question that he should have: "Am I qualified to operate the XYZ Company?" His answer would most likely have been yes because he was not only a risk-taker but also believed himself to be far more capable of handling problems than his previous experience indicated. Furthermore, I discovered later that this was not his first attempt to become a successful entrepreneur. Five years prior to the XYZ acquisition, he had purchased a small business on the side while he was still working full-time. The business showed some potential at first, but it failed within a year of its opening. I later discovered to my surprise that it failed not from the lack of absentee management but from an excess drain of available cash funds. The business was apparently well-managed, probably because John could only give it partial attention. But the excess drain on cash funds was clearly indicative of another characteristic of John's personality. He was a free spender and lived rather lavishly. He was a firm believer that money was to be used for spending and that the need to save for a rainy day was ridiculous. He had only one ambition in life, and that was to make as much money as possible in order to support his lifestyle. This quest for instant wealth overshadowed all sensible reasoning and without a doubt influenced his thinking regarding the management of the XYZ Company. He was so self-assured regarding his capability that his only preparation prior to becoming the leader within the group and one-third owner of the XYZ Company was a short and very concise seminar conducted by the Small Business Administration. During this seminar, he reviewed a publication titled *Thinking About Going into Business*. The pamphlet contained several questions people should ask themselves before going into business:

Summary

To start and run a small business you must know and be many things. As one small business owner attending a conference put it: "When I came here, my business lost the services of its chief executive, sales manager, controller, advertising department, personnel director, head bookkeeper, and janitor."

This aid booklet, based on questions asked by people in small business or contemplating starting, suggests the many facets of running a small concern that each owner-manager must become familiar with. While the answers to the questions are hardly exhaustive of any of the subjects, they provide the background for questions you may need to ask before going into business, as well as suggesting sources of answers to those questions.

Introduction

Almost everyone considering it has dozens of questions about starting a small business. The only foolish questions, of course, are the questions that aren't asked. Yet, many times we don't have enough information to ask the right questions.

The questions in this Aid Booklet are drawn from participants in satellite telecasts in thirteen states from New York to Mississippi. Most of the questioners didn't own, operate, or manage small businesses. Their questions are typical of what's on the minds of potential business owners. You may have pondered similar questions, as you thought about becoming your own boss.

The questions fell generally into areas such as the steps in setting up a business, business regulations and taxes, marketing, and financing a new concern. In this Aid Booklet the questions have been grouped by subject.

Answers to the questions came from experts in the various areas. These experts include a lawyer, an accountant, a bank loan officer, several small business owners, and market researchers.

These answers, it is hoped, will help you as you approach deciding on becoming a small business owner. The questions may suggest questions that you should find answers to before you invest your money, time, and effort in a small business.

Starting Out

1. If you have money but no particular business in mind, how can you get enough information on the best business to go into?

The best way of choosing your business venture is to look at your experience and educational background. A thorough review will provide leads on the business field you should enter—do what you know best. Even more important, you must like the business field you are going to enter to bring the enthusiasm and self-confidence you need to make the business go.

2.   What are the basic survival skills you need to run a business?

The basic survival skills include a working knowledge of basic recordkeeping; financial management; personnel management; market analysis; breakeven analysis; product or service knowledge; federal, state and local tax knowledge; legal structures; and communication skills.

3.   What special obstacles do women entering business face, and how can these obstacles be overcome?

Women are at last making inroads into business, not only as executives but as owners. There are many obstacles, chief among them the doubts that lenders, suppliers, and in some fields, customers have about women's ability to run businesses. These can be overcome with self-confidence and a strong belief in your ideas. You should not be discouraged by being rebuffed by people who simply don't understand. As more and more women enter business and succeed, the process will become easier and easier.

4.   What are the most important factors that cause small business failure?

There are, of course, many reasons for the failure of new small businesses. One way of looking at the causes is to remember that a new business is starting at zero momentum; newly entering a market, having to establish supplier relations, finding proper financing, and training employees. To coordinate all these facets and start them simultaneously is a tremendous job. If you don't have experience and management capability, success won't be very likely. You'll also find that undercapitalized businesses, those without enough cash to carry them through the first six months or so before the business starts making money, don't have good survival prospects. In such cases, even businesses with good management can founder.

5.   If you're trying to buy a going service business, how can you figure a reasonable price for the business that takes into account goodwill and business contacts in addition to the value of equipment and inventory?

There are many methods, but basically what you're trying to

do is set a value on the assets and earnings record of the firm. The simplest way is to determine the "payback period," usually two or three years. That is, the net profit for two years would equal the goodwill value. A more complicated and accurate method called the "net present value" method, is based on the cost of capital and a risk factor. For that method an accountant's help would be valuable.

6. What kind of a market study should you do before deciding to buy a radio station?

Determining the price of any business is difficult. For a radio station specifically, you can get the figures on the total revenue of all stations in the area (that is, advertising revenue) from the Federal Trade Commission. You should also get the percentage of the total market that the station you're considering has. You must also determine the potential market for the area in advertising dollars. Finding out the total number of businesses by line and size in the area covered by the station and their advertising expenditures would give you some insight. Really, you'd study the market like this for buying any business.

Regulations and Licenses

7. How do you find out what the federal, state, and local regulations are for the type of business you're going into?

The regulations for businesses may vary for different lines of business and certainly will from state to state. You can find out by contacting the various levels of government like the Internal Revenue Service for federal tax regulations, but your best bet is to go to your local SBA office. They can give you specific information for all levels of government. Local chambers of commerce can also often help you in this area.

8. What kind of registration and licenses are generally required?

Obviously, as we just discussed, there are specific requirements in each state and locality, but it is possible to list the kinds of basic licenses and registrations a new business will need:

LOCAL—A business license from city, town, or county,

depending on your location, will be necessary. In addition, you'll have to meet zoning laws, building codes, and similar regulations.

STATE—In most states, if your business isn't a corporation and your full name isn't in the name of the business, you'll have to register under what's called the fictitious name law. You should also file for a sales and use tax number. In some lines of business (like liquor stores, barber shops, real estate offices) specific licenses are needed.

FEDERAL—You'll need to contact the IRS for an employer's identification number and a "Going Into Business Tax Kit."

9.   What's this OSHA you hear about?

OSHA is the U.S. Labor Department's Occupational Safety and Health Administration. It is responsible for helping make work premises safe and healthy for employees. Since change in this area is frequent, it's best to contact OSHA itself. They have a number of publications aimed at small business.

10.   What are some specific legal requirements for mail order businesses which might not apply to other businesses?

The business under consideration would not use direct mail advertising, rather it would advertise in magazines and newspapers.

You should contact the Federal Trade Commission and get the FTC's list of publications; you can order those that pertain to your particular business. If you're selling food, you must get in touch with the Food and Drug Administration.

11.   How do you go about finding suppliers and manufacturers?

Most suppliers are interested in adding new accounts. A prime source for finding suppliers is the *Thomas Register*. It lists manufacturers by categories and geographical area. Most libraries have state's directory of manufacturers. If you know the product line and manufacturers, a letter or phone call to the companies will get you the local distributor-wholesaler. In some lines, trade shows are good sources of getting suppliers and looking over competing products.

12.   Should a sole proprietor with no employees have disability benefits?

If you can afford it, it's a good idea. It makes sense to protect the income of a small sole proprietorship with income maintenance insurance. Ask your insurance agent about various plans.

13.   How often should a small grocery store take an inventory?

A physical (can by can) inventory should be taken at least once a quarter. If your fiscal year ended December 31, you'd take one then and subsequently on March 31, June 30, September 30, and so on. If you have an automated ordering system, you can take a physical inventory less frequently.

14.   How long does it take a new business to establish a good public image?

A good public image takes a long time to establish (and only minutes to lose). There is no set formula, but a good image depends on:

> The service, products, and customer treatment you provide;
>
> The market you're in;
>
> How you stack up against your competitors;
>
> The quality of your public relations and advertising programs. If you're new to a market—and if you do what you say you're going to—you may establish an excellent reputation in 18 to 24 months.

15.   How do you find a good lawyer?

As with most personal services, you must have rapport with your attorney. The best way to determine this is to talk to lawyers by phone or visit them before you make a selection. Get recommendations from friends, your banker, or lastly a "lawyers' reference service." You're looking for someone you can trust and who will take an interest in you and your business.

16.   Do you need a lawyer to start a business?

No, but it's wise to get the best advice possible when you're starting out. An attorney is one source of the expertise you'll

need to draw on. In some states you need an attorney to form
a corporation. Check your state law.

Form of Business

17.   What form of business do you recommend for a new
business?

Each legal form, sole proprietorship, partnership, or corporation, has its advantages and disadvantages. The one you
should pick depends on your circumstances, including:

Your financial condition,

The line of business you're entering,

The number of employees,

The risk involved,

Your tax situation.

Don't assume, if you plan a one-person business, that sole
proprietorship is the way to go. See your lawyer.

18.   I've heard that the Subchapter S corporation and "1244"
stock offerings are designed for small business. Could you
explain them?

Essentially, a Subchapter S corporation treats profits or losses
by the corporation as ordinary income or loss to the individual stockholder. A full discussion of the Subchapter S
corporation can be found in Internal Revenue Service Publication Number 589.

Internal Revenue Code Section 1244 allows an individual to
treat losses on the stock of a "small business corporation"
as deductions against ordinary income. IRS Publication
Numbers 542, 544, and 550 have sections discussing this
regulation.

The rules for taking advantage of these devices are quite specific and a little involved. You should get the IRS publications. You can get copies by getting in touch with your local
IRS office. It's listed in your local directory under "U.S. Government." It would be a good idea to discuss these topics
with your accountant, lawyer, or other business advisor.

19.   Is it a good idea to incorporate your business in a state
other than the one in which you plan to do business?

No. For small businesses it's normally best to incorporate where you are going to do business. If you incorporate out of state, you'd have to register as a "foreign" corporation.

Taxes

20.   Is a sales person, paid on a commission basis, treated like an hourly wage sales clerk with respect to tax withholding?

Yes, unless the sales person is a manufacturer's rep or is in business as an independent contractor.

21.   Concerning a sales representative on straight commission, is it mandatory to take out FICA taxes (social security) and withholding taxes?

Yes, if the rep is an employee of the company. The deciding factor is whether or not the rep is an independent contractor in business for herself or himself.

22.   What about casual labor and taxes?

If an individual is your employee, you must withhold taxes. The only exception is if the labor is on an independent contract basis. Then the independent contractor withholds taxes and files all appropriate forms.

23.   Say you have a partnership between two people and the spouse of one of the partners keeps the books, is the spouse an employee, even if he or she isn't paid?

If he or she weren't paid, such a bookkeeper could be classified as a nonemployee. Thus, since there are no wages, there are no withholdings for income tax, FICA, and the like. If you paid him or her, it would be like any other employee for tax purposes.

24.   If I live in one state but go to other states to sell goods, how do I handle taxes?

As a business in another state, you'd have to collect and remit taxes to the state where the goods are sold. Most states have forms to remit these collected taxes. These sales should be kept separate from sales in your home state, since you would not pay home state tax on them.

25.   How is a corporation taxed if all stockholders work as

salaried employees and all profits are applied to the liquidation of the original purchase debt?

Stockholding employees are taxed on salaries like any other employee. The purchase price of a corporation is not a debt to the corporation, but an investment by the stockholders who bought the business. Thus, profits can't be used to liquidate this price. Profits may be used to retire corporate debts and thus increase net worth, but all principal payments are taxable profits and taxed according to the corporate tax structure. If your net earnings before taxes approach $100,000, check with the IRS. It may be necessary to pay dividends, since nonpayment could be considered a technique for avoiding dividend taxation.

The Market

26.   How can you get the census data you need to estimate the market for your store or service in a given locality?

You can get census information from the Bureau of the Census in the U.S. Department of Commerce, as well as through chambers of commerce and various state and local agencies that deal with business. You can find this information in your local public library and get it from nearby colleges and universities, too.

27.   How can you find out what the prevailing costs are for a service business in your market area?

One way is simply to call competitors and ask their prices. Their prices will give you a lead. You could ask competitors' customers for the same information if you didn't want to go directly to the competition.

28.   How do you go about determining the market for a mail order business?

The principles of determining market share and market potential are the same no matter how large the geographical area. You must first determine a customer profile, the size of the market, and the number of competitors. You could also use a readership survey given to you by a magazine in which you intend to advertise.

Pricing

29. How do you figure markup and markdown?

Markup (Markon) is the original amount that the merchandise is marked up. Markup as a percentage (also called gross margin rate) is figured as a percentage of sales. For example, say the cost of merchandise is $10 and you want a 20 percent markup; what is the selling price (SP)? By definition we know that markup as a percentage is given as a percentage of sales. Thus, our cost must be 80 percent of the selling price (100 percent selling price − 20 percent desired markup).

The formula is:

$$SP = \frac{Cost}{Cost \ as \ \% \ of \ SP}$$

$$SP = \frac{\$10.00}{.80}$$

$$SP = \$12.50$$

So, our selling price is $12.50: cost of $10.00 and markup $2.50 or 20 percent of the selling price.

Markdown (discount) is a reduction of selling price below the original sale price. Assume the item is marked down to $11.25. The markdown is $1.25 or a 10 percent markdown ($1.25 markdown divided by $12.50 original selling price).

30. How would you go about establishing price guidelines for a business renting items to customers?

Pricing is based normally on a combination of cost and market competition. Trade associations are a prime source of such information. Check your library for the Encyclopedia of Associations with which you'll be able to find the association dealing with your business.

Finances

31. What is the average expected net profit for small business?

Average net profits vary with the type of business—retail, wholesale, service, manufacturing, construction. They also vary for the type of business structure—proprietorship or corporation. Dun & Bradstreet and Robert Morris Associates publish ratios which give you these figures, as well as lots of very useful cost information.

32.   Would you explain the meaning of "rate of return on investment"? How is it different from net profit? Is it different from return on assets employed?

Net profit (before taxes) is basically total sales for a specific period less cost of goods and operating expenses during that period. (For a retail business, cost of goods would be your cost of merchandise sold.) Net profit is a function of both rate of return on investment (ROI) and return on total assets. ROI is net profit divided by capital invested by the owners of the company.

ROI is used to measure the effectiveness of management in attaining the owners' desired return on their investment. Generally, the larger the ROI, the more attractive a company is to potential investors.

Return on total assets is the net profit divided by total assets. This measures the net profitability of the use of all resources of the business. It is another tool for measuring management effectiveness in the use of all resources borrowed and equity.

33.   Does a bank require absolute top credit references from loan applicants?

The better the credit references the greater possibility of loan approval.

34.   If I estimate my start-up cost at $50,000 and can't put up anywhere near the $25,000 that I've been told is what I should have for my share, am I wasting my time even filling out a loan application?

In all probability you would be, although there are some exceptions. For example, it might be possible to get a loan under your circumstances if you were buying a business that's already operating well enough to provide sufficient profits to cover its obligations and the loan. Furthermore, if the applicant is the present manager who has made this business go, the chances of getting such a loan are much better.

Help!

35.   Getting money is difficult; keeping it may be even more difficult. Where can I get assistance in managing my business?

Your accountant and bank can provide financial counseling which can be very helpful in starting and managing your business. They can also give you invaluable information on the local area and your market that can be crucial in making decisions in your business.*

I have no criticism of the SBA questionnaire booklet, but it certainly does not provide enough information or preparation for anyone to assume the risk of spending $100,000 of their own money, pledging an additional $600,000, and involving two other associates in the same venture. Without a doubt, John's desire for money was his sole objective in life. The means for achieving it was of little consequence. As we will learn later, the XYZ Company became that means.

Tom sold his small accounting firm to become treasurer and secretary of the XYZ Company. The firm had enjoyed a moderate growth over a five-year period under his direction, but was never able to capture some of the more larger and lucrative clients. During his five years in public accounting rumors, concerning certain unethical associations with clients continually surfaced with respect to Tom's practice, but nothing was ever proven. As a person, Tom was so different from John that it is hard to understand how the two individuals ever became partners. Tom was no dreamer and certainly not a risk-taker. All his actions were carefully evaluated before being taken. He joined the XYZ team for the same reason as John, to make money, but he harbored no illusions about how to achieve his monetary objectives. Seizing any opportunity to make money that might come his way was Tom's philosophy on life and the basis for all his actions. Of the three principles, Tom had

*Excerpted from the U.S. Small Business Administration Management Aid Booklet No. 2.025 "Thinking About Going Into Business?" Reprinted April, 1981.

the more dominant personality. But he was shrewd enough to let John take the lead, accepting the lessor role of an armchair quarterback and therefore never having to take the entire blunt of criticism resulting from a poor business decision. But he was also ready and able to seize the initiative if it benefited his purpose.

Despite these obvious differences, John and Tom both respected one another. For John, Tom represented the cool and calculating person who always seems to know what he is doing. For Tom, John was the risk-taker he would never be. Although he truly admired John's happy-go-lucky attitude, it simply was not in his personality to assume such a flamboyant posture.

Of the three principals, Bob was perhaps the most qualified from an operational standpoint. As a former employee prior to the acquisition, he was familiar with the operations within the company from its inception to its present acquisition as the XYZ Company. He had started with the company at an early age and had worked himself gradually up to the position of general manager prior to the acquisition. He had hoped someday to be able to acquire the company himself, but he lacked sufficient funds to be considered a serious buyer and his dreams were shattered by the acquisition takeover. For this reason, his relationship with the other two principals was clouded by some jealousy and considerable distrust. Frankly, he was bitter over missing his opportunity to own the company he had worked for all his life. His distrust for both John and Tom was based on the nagging question of why they allowed him to buy at least one-third of the business knowing that he had tried to acquire the entire operation prior to the three-way acquisition. The truth was that both John and Tom believed that Bob's influence as a former employee would help stabilize the company over the next few years. If Bob failed as a constructive team player during this period, they planned to force him to leave by buying his shares. Thus Bob had every reason to be concerned about his future, but he had no idea of John's and Tom's intentions.

As you can see from the differences in the personalities of the three principals, the XYZ Company was a potential fuse, waiting to be ignited by any one of the three principals.

Before I detail the events leading XYZ to the brink of bankruptcy, let's quickly review the XYZ's status on the eve of the acquisition:

John had no experience as an entrepreneur. Furthermore, he underestimated the complexity of becoming a business owner and was more of an idealist than a realist. To make money was his goal at XYZ—everything else would follow as a natural consequence.

Tom was an opportunist who would quickly cut down the other two principals if it served his purpose to make money.

Bob was bitter over having to share what he thought was going to be his company. Starting now, he secretly vowed it would be a race between him and his two associates to gain full control over the XYZ Company.

Although I have already indicated that the XYZ Company was a solid acquisition with potential growth in new markets, it was not entirely void of all problems. For example, 20 percent of its inventory at the time of acquisition was obsolete. Three key pieces of equipment essential to the defense market needed either major overhaul or replacement. There were no job standards in the manufacturing operation but there was an employees' union that enjoyed strong support among the workers. Automation was something everyone talked about but nobody could understand how to apply to XYZ. Considering how little experience the three principal shareholders had before the acquisition, it is doubtful that they would have established a plan of action to resolve these problems even if they had been aware of their existence. The most obvious reason these problems had failed to come to their attention was their failure to develop an initial cash projection. Tom should have taken the lead in this area as part of his financial duties, but no one raised any questions about the need for this type of projection, so he conveniently allowed the matter to go unnoticed rather than create additional work for himself that he felt no one would appreciate or understand anyway.

Despite their lack of experience and their indifference to XYZ's problems, the operation moved forward with very few problems because it was being directed by the two previous managers. For both the XYZ Company and the three principals, this arrangement could not have been better; the company continued to prosper and grow as if no acquisition had ever taken place, and John, Tom, and Bob were free to pursue own, more interesting objectives. John bought an expensive automobile and home. He traveled constantly around the country in an effort to acquire new customers. He was only partially successful in developing new markets, but his expense account was a little bit short of the national debt. In the meantime, Tom had acquired a new lease on life, or at least two lives, one with his present wife and the other with a newfound girlfriend. While all this was happening, Bob was laying the groundwork to undermine both John and Tom.

At this time the only action necessary to ignite their volatile arrangement was the departure of the two previous managers. And on February 25, 1978—one year after the acquisition, in accordance with the provisions of their initial contract—the two previous key managers left the XYZ Company in the hands of its new owners.

John's first decision after one full year as president was to make an attempt to persuade the two former key managers to return to the XYZ Company. Although he failed to convince them, this first real decision showed good judgment. His next decision, however, would eventually lead to the ultimate collapse of XYZ Company. John had no intention of returning to the company to assume the role of a full-time president, for two reasons. He knew by this time that he was not experienced enough to handle the job and therefore had no wish to call attention to himself by returning to XYZ as president. Furthermore, he was enjoying his assignment of developing new marketing contacts, especially the travel, the lavish meals, and the people he met. In effect, he was living the type of lifestyle that he enjoyed and the XYZ Company was picking up the tab. The results of his efforts, however, showed that he was a better entertainer than salesperson. After failing to convince the two former owners to return, he appointed Tom to the position of chief executive officer with complete authority to direct the operations of the company during his absence.

Tom was overjoyed by John's decision. It gave him the opportunity to operate the company in a manner that could serve his own personal needs. For him, the timing of the decision was perfect: over the last few months his personal funds had being drained by the life he was leading. With the new appointment, he now felt justified in giving himself a sizable salary increase. Bob's reaction to John's decision was also predictable. With John constantly traveling and not performing his duties as president, Bob could concentrate on eliminating Tom.

Six months after John's decision, the XYZ Company began to feel the first shock waves of what would eventually become a major cash flow problem. The balance of cash on hand was not sufficient enough to meet the weekly employee payroll. Tom quickly rectified the shortage by requesting a short-term note from the bank, and the first warning of impending cash problems was then forgotten.

The second shock wave, however, raised more concern. XYZ failed to pay two bank installments, and the bank suddenly focused attention on XYZ's activities for the first time since the acquisition. Tom was immediately requested to submit an updated profit and loss statement. He in turn requested the accounting firm to comply with the bank's request. At the time the request was made, the accounting firm was in the middle of its year-end tax season with more work than it could handle. It did respond to Tom's request as quickly as possible but in the interim the available cash funds continued to drop very rapidly. Finally, in May, the accounting firm submitted an updated financial statement for the company's activities as of the end of March. The bank reviewed the financial information very carefully and submitted a letter to the XYZ Company expressing concern over its assessment of the statements. For the first time, the XYZ Company was told by way of the bank's financial review that it had some serious cash flow problems. For example, sales had dropped 25 percent over the last six months while expenses had increased by 15 percent. Working capital had dropped to such a low level that the bank was concerned about XYZ's ability to meet its bank obligations over the next six months.

The bank was quite concerned about the considerable financial deterioration XYZ had shown. Furthermore, the financial statement only reflected activity up to the end of March, leaving April and May open for question. Tom was called on to meet with the bank on three different occasions over the next two weeks. The Bank demanded some answers, including a detailed explanation of what XYZ was going to do about the current state of affairs. Of course, Tom was caught off-guard. Over the last six months as the newly appointed CEO, he had spent less time reviewing the company financial condition than he had given to reading his morning newspaper. There was no way that he was going to accept the blame for XYZ's poor performance. He was far too clever to deliberately become the bank's only target for criticism. What he needed was a scapegoat. He could not blame John without jeopardizing his position within the company, so the logical choice was Bob. As a result, all his answers to the bank's questions were carefully orchestrated to put the blame on Bob. For example, sales had dropped due to a lack of bookings, but John was not blamed for his poor showing: it was Bob's fault for not being able to make deliveries on time. And expense increases, which had actually resulted from excessive spending, were blamed on poor performance in the plant.

The solution to resolving the current financial problems was also cleverly handled by Tom. Bob would be asked to sell his shares to a friend of Tom's who was considered an experienced venture capitalist with considerable cash. At first the bank was skeptical of Tom's response but it had a sizable outstanding loan with XYZ to protect. Consequently, it agreed to accept Tom's plan on one condition: if Tom succeeded in bringing into the XYZ Company a new shareholder with venture capital, one-third of the current balance of the bank loan would be due and the new shareholder would have to agree to sign a new bank note along with John and Tom, covering the remaining balance due from XYZ. Tom was delighted at having won at least the first round. John was told about the matter but could see no serious problems that might involve him and therefore gave his consent to the plan. At first, Bob was furious. Not only had he been tagged as the scapegoat but now he was being asked to sell his shares and leave XYZ. When he finally calmed down he began to rationally assess his situation within the company. It now appeared hopeless that he could ever gain control over the entire company. He could not continue to work with the two other shareholders, knowing how they felt about him. His image at the bank had been compromised, thanks to Tom. So Bob finally decided to accept Tom's plan and leave before any further problems within XYZ materialized.

It was an emotional wrench for Bob to leave XYZ after so many years of service, but on March 20th, a little over a year after the acquisition of XYZ Company, he sold his entire interest in the company to the new shareholder and friend of Tom, George. Considering what was to come, Bob's decision to leave was perhaps the best thing ever to happen to him.

George was a professional investor in every sense of the word. Over the years he had made similar investments in other business operations with a successful track record of eventual takeover of the entire business. Compared to John and Bob, whose actions could only be considered superficial and amateur, he was a proven master at the art of taking over businesses, and takeover was exactly what he had in mind for the XYZ Company. His plan was so simple that even a college freshman majoring in business would have been able to follow his reasoning. His plan was to continue to invest just enough cash to keep XYZ Company afloat, but to withhold the necessary funds to bring it completely back to a healthy operation. This would allow the XYZ Company to continue to weaken gradually, while George's investment in the company eventually exceeded the equity positions of both John and Tom. For the next six months activity at the XYZ Company seemed, at least on the surface, to be stabilized. In reality, XYZ was no better off than it had been six months earlier, but with the continual influx of just enough cash from George, the company was able to cover its continual cash drain. John did not care what was happening by this time as long as he was allowed to continue to wine and dine potential customers. George's plan of eventual takeover was therefore right on schedule and seemed to be inevitable. However, neither George nor John was aware of what Tom was now doing.

As you may recall, Tom had been living with and supporting his wife and girlfriend at the same time. The financial burden had become so heavy that his present salary could no longer support his lifestyle. By mid-1978, he was already in serious debt and had started to play games with the Internal Revenue Service and the state with respect to XYZ's tax liabilities. His plan was simple and for a while, at least, workable. On the other hand it was a dangerous, stupid, and losing proposition. But it could be initiated without John or George being aware of it. As the financial officer of the company, Tom would sign the payroll tax returns, make the checks payable to cash, cash them, and send the return in to the IRS without the check. The reason the scheme was effective for a considerable period of time was partially because of the time it took the Internal Revenue Service to investigate the discrepancy.

The first communication Tom received from the Internal Revenue was a notice requesting an explanation. The second notice, which arrived a few months later, was more direct:

> We have sent you several notices and demands for payment of the Federal taxes shown at the end of this letter, but we have no record of receiving the amount due. This is your final notice that the taxes are overdue and the total amount you owe must be paid within 10 days from the date of this letter.
>
> If you recently paid the amount due but your payment has not been credited to your account, or if you cannot pay all you owe, contact us at the above number. Otherwise, make your check or money order payable to the Internal Revenue Service and be sure it has your employer identification on it. The number is shown above. Then send your payment with the copy of this letter attached so we can promptly and accurately credit your account.
>
> An envelope is provided for your convenience.
>
> If we do not hear from you within the 10-day period, enforcement actions may be taken to pay these taxes without further notice to you. These actions may include filing a notice of Federal tax lien to give your creditors public notice of a lien against your property; serving your employer a notice of levy against your salary or wages; levying your bank accounts, receivables, commissions, or any other income you have; and seizing and selling your property or rights to property, such as automobiles.

By this time it should have been apparent to Tom that he was becoming trapped by his own actions into a no-win situation. But he took no action to rectify the matter. In retrospect I am not sure if he knew what to do or if he was afraid to do anything. Nevertheless, within 10 days of receiving the warning letter from the Internal Revenue a lien was promptly placed on all XYZ's assets. The following day we were requested by XYZ's bank to review and assess the company's problems and given a mandate to provide them with preliminary recommendations within seven days.

When we arrived at the XYZ Company, exactly two years and 45 days after its acquisition, everyone was in a state of shock. The operations in the plant had stopped so suddenly that it was as if someone had simply turned off the power. John was stranded in California, with no money to pay his airfare home. Tom had simply left the office and no one knew where he had gone. George was not accepting any telephone calls and had all messages referred to his attorney. All the machinery in the plant had been tagged by the Internal Revenue Service. Some of the workers were still at the plant asking about the wages due them for the last week's work. When I walked into the plant with a loan officer from the bank, I was not quite sure whether the few remaining people would welcome us as friends or hang us as enemies.

On April 16, 1979, with no prior knowledge of any of the events I have just described, we began one of the most difficult assignments I can remember. Within the allotted seven-day period we quickly assessed the XYZ Company and presented the following findings to the bank.

1. XYZ Company had been completely shut down by the Internal Revenue Service for failure to pay payroll tax delinquencies, estimated to be approximately $75,000 plus penalties and interest.
2. A quick assessment of the financial records supplied by the accounting firm showed a gradual deterioration in bookings, profits, and working capital over the last six months.
3. The current outstanding debt to vendors and others was approximated at $60,000. This amount did not

include the $75,000 of tax liability or the bank loan with a current balance due of $500,000.

4. Current assets were estimated at $50,000, representing mostly uncollected accounts receivables. There was a small cash balance of $2,000. All equipment had been liened by the Internal Revenue Service until the tax liability was paid.

5. John, the absentee President of XYZ Company, had returned from California to his home. He was unable to offer any constructive suggestions to resolve the problem that XYZ Company was facing. His attitude was a combination of disbelief, shock, and severe depression and concern over what to expect in the next few months.

6. Tom was finally located at his summer residence but refused to talk to us.

7. We were also unable to contact George but managed to speak with his attorney, who was preparing to sue the XYZ Company on behalf of his client for misappropriation of funds.

In summary, the bank was due to lose $500,000, and the Internal Revenue Service intended to recover the outstanding $75,000 plus penalties even if it took every last penny from the XYZ Company, all the personal assets of the three principals, as well as if necessary, payments from each one of them for the rest of their lives or until the taxes were paid. We advised the bank that it had only two choices: write off the $500,000 debt or invest additional money in a reorganization effort to place the XYZ Company back into business. However, we could not offer any assurances that a reorganization plan would be successful.

The bank deliberated for three days, during which the details of our preliminary report were carefully reviewed. On the fourth day, we were asked to meet with several key bank loan officers. During this meeting, the bank informed us that

they were not prepared to write off the $500,000 and re-
quested that we prepare an alternative plan of action with
an estimated cost of implementation. Within the week we
submitted a plan to the bank for consideration which included the following provisions:

1. The bank would pay the tax liability of $75,000 plus
    penalties in order to remove all liens on XYZ assets
    (including machinery).
2. At this point the bank would then have the option to
    sell the XYZ's assets and seize the personal assets col-
    lateralized by the three principals on the bank note
    in order to recover what we estimated to be a net gain
    of $150,000 determined as follows:

Current Outstanding Bank Loan	$500,000
Estimated Payment of Delinquent Taxes	75,000
Total Payout	**$425,000**
Less:	
Sales of XYZ Machinery	36,000
Collection of Accounts Receivable	50,000
Auction off Personal Assets of the Three Principals, John, Tom, and George	165,000
Total Recovery	**$515,000**
Net Gain	**$150,000**

On paper this option, at first glance, offered the bank an
attractive means to recover the outstanding debt. But there
were many minus sides to this action which we called to
the bank's attention. First of all, the XYZ Company had not
declared bankruptcy or initiated any actions to redirect its
present state of affairs. This was undoubtedly due to John's
present state of mind, which left him paralyzed and unable

to comprehend or react to the plight of the XYZ Company. Furthermore, this option carried many legal ramifications that would have to be considered before proceeding.

What we were attempting to inform the bank of was that specific actions could be taken, but that the process would be time-consuming and have no guarantee of success. In our opinion, there were no quick solutions to this dilemma.

While we were working with the bank in an attempt to salvage something from the pending XYZ collapse, other events were occurring at the same time. For example, George started legal action against the XYZ Company and the other two principals, John and Tom, for misrepresentation of the company's position prior to his acquisition and misappropriation of company funds during the time he was a shareholder. The bank started to receive threatening calls from XYZ workers who had not been paid before the plant had been closed. John became ill and was admitted to the hospital for tests.

Meanwhile, the Internal Revenue Service was trying to contact Tom regarding the current tax liabilities. Failure to pay payroll taxes was considered a serious matter by the IRS. As an employer the XYZ Company—and Tom as its principal financial officer—was the trustee of the employee's payroll taxes and was responsible for the withholding tax and social security collected from each employee. Therefore, when Tom used this money for his personal purposes the IRS considered this an improper action which could not only lead to the assessment of penalties and interest but also constitute intent to defraud the government, which if proved could mean a charge of criminal felony and result in a possible one-year prison sentence. Along with the IRS, we contacted Tom by phone to inform him of the IRS's position and their need to talk with him. He was very abusive to us and threatened to shoot the first person who stepped foot on his property. I discussed the matter with the IRS agents on the case and decided that he was just bluffing. On the following Tuesday morning after our initial telephone call,

I drove to Tom's residence, parked the car in the driveway, and started to walk toward the front door. About half-way up the steps I suddenly stopped, frozen in my tracks by the sound of two shots fired over my head from Tom's house. Two hours later, three federal marshals arrested Tom and drove him to the courthouse, where he was booked at the county jail and later released on bail.

The only promising event to happen during this time was a call we received from Bob, the former principal who had sold his interest to George several months before. He requested that we ask the bank how much personal investment they would require from him to finance his efforts to gain control of the XYZ Company. The bank was caught off-guard by this request. Their thinking up to this point had been centered on how to recover their debt, not on how to support another individual in his efforts to reestablish a company already "on the rocks."

By this time, we were not the only professionals involved in this chaotic abyss. The bank was consulting with its attorneys. Each of the three principals had engaged the services of attorneys. And finally, each attorney was being advised by different accounting firms. This gridlock of confusion was finally ended by John, who, acting as president of the XYZ Company, filed for bankruptcy on November 20, 1979 under Chapter 11 of the bankruptcy code. The court immediately appointed a trustee and placed the XYZ Company in Chapter 11, a legal structure prior to bankruptcy that allows a company a certain specified period of time to reorganize its current state of financial affairs in order to avoid the final act of bankruptcy under Chapter 13 of the bankruptcy code.

At this point in our story let's take a moment and recapitulate the position of each party involved with the XYZ Company.

1. The XYZ Company has now been placed under the direction of a court-appointed trustee assigned to the task of reconstructing the financial affairs of the com-

pany. The trustee appointed by the court was one of the three loan officers of the bank that had initially engaged our consulting firm.

2. All three principals were now fully engaged in negotiations with the IRS over the payment of delinquent payroll taxes. By this time, however, both John and Tom were personally bankrupt, leaving George with the only cash funds available to pay the delinquent taxes. George's legal action against the XYZ Company had failed to discourage the Internal Revenue Service in its efforts to collect the outstanding tax liability. Tom's legal problems with the IRS still remained to be resolved, but it was becoming more apparent each day that the IRS would be willing to drop any further actions with Tom if the taxes could be collected from George. It was obvious that the IRS did not intend to pursue any actions that would not result in the immediate collection of the existing tax liability. Therefore, George had become involved in the past due tax problem despite his attempt to avoid the issue. According to the IRS, he was equally responsible along with the two other principals for the actions of the XYZ Company and, furthermore, the only principal left in the company with enough cash reserves to satisfy the judgment.

3. In the meantime, Bob's efforts to acquire the XYZ Company were being considered by the court-appointed trustee. The major stumbling block preventing Bob from becoming a serious alternative was his lack of a formal plan, clearly defining his objectives with supporting schedules showing cash projections of how much money he would need to borrow, how much money he was willing to invest, and how he planned to repay the bank loan.

It was obvious to the bank that they were now faced with about the same options we had presented before the court had placed the XYZ Company into Chapter 11: that is, allow the XYZ Company to file for bankruptcy and accept the consequences of a reduced reimbursement for the outstanding loan or consider another entrepreneur to back, like Bob, who felt sure he could bring the XYZ Company back to its initial profitability. Furthermore, there was no way the bank could continually direct the operating responsibilities of XYZ. We were requested by the bank and the court trustee to submit our recommendations within 30 days.

Ordinarily, we try to make every effort when humanly possible to prevent any business from going bankrupt by implementing what we call a program of last resort. However, in the case of the XYZ Company, we concluded that any effort to resolve the present state of affairs would require a miracle. To give you a better understanding why we felt justified in our decision, let me describe the level of complexity and the enormous effort required to implement successfully a program of last resort before going bankrupt. As defined in my recent book *The Action-Step Plan to Avoiding Business Bankruptcy:*

> The first step taken by the business consultant is the assessment of your existing business condition. This requires that the consultant determine as quickly as possible if the operation can be salvaged and what steps can be taken to stop any further deterioration.
>
> Available cash reserves are the focal point during this determination. A continual drain on cash reserves can lead to a total shutdown of operations along with a cutoff of available funds to pay ongoing expenses. Therefore, all sources of incoming cash and committed disbursements should be quickly reviewed. For example, if outstanding receivables are six months overdue, the accounts receivable balance must be reviewed to determine what action is necessary to collect the money. Sometimes, a review also reveals excessively high payrolls coupled with idle time and low productivity; if so an immediate cut in the total work force may be warranted.
>
> Recognizing problems is comparatively simple, but finding

solutions never is. An assessment program is implemented step by step.

Profits

Profits are recognized as a common factor leading to success or failure and the one most often pointed to when businesses do fail. It is also the factor that is the most difficult to control because of its reliance on the success or failure of other business factors, such as sales volume, level of expense activity, and one-time expenses. Nevertheless, there are several specific action-steps that do govern the general makeup of profit even though it is much broader than some of the other areas in the success or failure column.

Profits can be increased for any business once the business has an established cash-projection program, financial and operating controls are in place, and management demonstrates an ability to plan ahead. Without planning, controls, and an adequate accounting record, cash reserves can be drained without the knowledge of the owner. If the operation reaches a point where cash profits are insufficient to carry forward the normal operations of the business, immediate action by the business consultant must be taken to turn the business around. These steps include: checking all sources of available cash (banks, friends, savings, personal assets, etc.), freezing all further variable expenses at the source of commitment, and reducing the size of the operation and the fixed overhead.

Most business owners will usually give permission to take whatever steps are necessary to find additional sources of money and even permit steps to restrict the existing disbursements within their operation. Few business owners will agree to a reduction of their present size even though it is much easier to live with a bruised ego than the consequences of bankruptcy. As you can see, these action steps of last resort are far more severe than the establishment of a cash-control program to aid the business owner in maintaining a consistent control over profits. However, the establishment of programs for long-range planning of cash, expense, and operational controls are the necessary cornerstones for continuous success once the steps of last resort have been implemented.

Collections

If one were to ask the average business owner today what his or her greatest problem is, the answer would reflect the inability to collect from customers. Restrictions of available cash funds among the general business community has become so severe that collecting cash has become the major problem for all business owners.

A cash collection program must include increasing the turnover rate of accounts receivable, restricting credit to all but acknowledged paying customers, instituting cash-on-delivery terms where necessary, acquiring cash advances before the work is completed to cover fixed overhead, and initiating a rapid billing process.

Although it is no secret that any collection program will add to the existing cash reserves, most owners have no established procedures for collecting outstanding receivables. Why should this paradox be allowed to exist when cash problems are so obvious? Naturally, there are many reasons why the average business owner doesn't like to enforce a collection policy. The most common reason given is the possibility of losing the good will of particular customers by pressing them too hard to pay overdue invoices. In other cases, some owners simply can't bring themselves to ask customers to pay their bills. There are others who operate with a total disregard for the need to collect until they find themselves without cash.

The professional must move quickly to modify the existing collection policy or establish one if the operation is without one. The first step is to reclassify existing receivables into collectibles and noncollectibles. The latter are written off as bad debts. The classification of a receivable as noncollectible is the result of an exhausting effort on the part of the business owner who exercises every means available from collection agencies to the threat of legal action but still fails to collect the monies due. In short, the customer has no money to pay you or assets that you can repossess to satisfy the debt. Contact is then made with those who are believed to be collectible. An approach by the professional manager is usually more successful in eliciting the owed monies because the professional represents a third party and is therefore taken more seriously. Generally, an attempt is made to establish a payment plan only if there is no other choice. As a rule of thumb, the collection effort endeavors to keep the customer's good will, but pressure will be exerted when there is no other alternative. The pressure itself can take many forms depending on the size of the outstanding invoice and what leverage the owner has over future dealings with the customer. Most business owners feel that suing the customer for the amount due is the last alternative. Other types of actions are more subtle, such as holding up existing shipments or threatening to put the customer on a C.O.D. basis on the next order. But whatever course is taken, diplomacy is the key to a proper collection policy.

The entire process becomes one of negotiating with the customer, and this often can best be accomplished by a professional. In my own experience, I have found that most people want to pay after an acceptable payment plan is agreed upon by both parties.

Once the initial steps are taken to make the collection process more effective, a permanent program should be put in place that encompasses advance payment for partially completed work, C.O.D. terms for new customers, a more thorough and aggressive credit policy for questionable customers, a continual program of review and analysis of the existing open receivable accounts, and a stepped-up billing procedure.

Bookings

At first blush, problems with bookings seem elementary. Increased bookings means additional cash revenues; a decrease in bookings can place a drain on existing cash reserves. A continual drop in bookings should be taken very seriously because it is generally symptomatic of deeper problems within the marketing organization of the business. Surprisingly, a drop in bookings often comes as a shock to the client. At first, no discernible effects are felt because cash is not immediately affected. Thus the problem tends to be ignored.

However, the professional's steps of last resort presume that the basic problems causing the fall-off in bookings exist within your marketing program. Actions aimed at solving the immediate difficulty involve steps such as sales promotion to reduce the inventory of slow-moving lines in order to gain some needed funds, but long-range programs must be instituted too. Any such permanent solution is based on a thorough assessment by the professional of the owner's existing marketing policies. All marketing factors are evaluated from pricing to actions of the competition.

It has been my experience that an increase in bookings is directly related to an effort to upgrade and revise the direction of marketing. Conversely, owners with booking problems never establish marketing programs or allow existing ones to drift without updating or redirection.

Once you have implemented the steps of last resort in the marketing area, mass promotional efforts coupled with drastic reduction in price of certain products can be only temporary measures to bring in additional funds. More steps are needed to lay the groundwork for a sound marketing program.

Investors

One way for a business to acquire additional cash is to sell stock to investors. For the small business operation, this action has always been subjected to various preconditions. For example, a closely held family-owned corporation is limited as to the amount of stock it can sell without losing control of its business. For those who own their businesses outright as sole proprietors, there are no shares of stock to sell, even though many of these sole proprietors eventually reach a stage where growth and expansion require substantial funds that can no longer be funded by personal investments. For still other operations the need for additional funds may require that they consider going public by placing stock on the open market. Though the process of going public is complex and not recommended as a do-it-yourself exercise, it is the objective of many family-owned corporations. The cash rewards can be substantial, provided that the action is well planned and directed by a qualified professional.

Even during times of economic downturn, there are still many people with money to invest who wait for the right opportunities to come along. The task of convincing investors that your business offers them a viable opportunity, regardless of the economy, is far from easy. It becomes an even more difficult feat to attract investors if your business is in trouble.

The job of locating investors willing to accept a high risk is difficult, and therefore a judgment should be made by a professional who knows if an investor is interested in your operation.

Many businesses are viewed by the investors as too far gone to be turned around by a simple infusion of money. A prudent investor usually completes a thorough review of the business before money is invested. With the aid of professionals, potential investors attempt to determine how the business got into trouble and why it was allowed to happen. This question can be answered only by a complete assessment of the business owner's capabilities as an effective manager of his or her operations. Some investors can be attracted or turned off simply by the product or services the troubled business has to offer. A product or service that has current market appeal can be more interesting to the potential investor because he or she can see possibilities coupled perhaps with a few management changes in the investment. It is good to remember two simple rules in this area: (1) if your business is to continue to grow, investors are sources of additional funds, and (2) if your business is undercapitalized, investors can represent not only additional cash funds but also a source of new talent to aid you in building a management team.

Inventory

. . . I mentioned that higher inventory turnover increases cash flow while lower turnover rates decrease available cash. What was not discussed is what steps a professional can take to solve an inventory problem.

The first step is to classify the existing inventory stock in terms of high-moving items and items that have not moved and become obsolete. The next step is to sell as much of the obsolete inventory as is possible.

There are three basic reasons for these steps: (1) the sale of obsolete inventory provides additional cash with little or no risk of reducing profitable inventory items from stock, (2) inventory on the shelf for a long period of time restricts available cash that could be used for other purposes, and (3) shelves cleared of obsolete goods offer additional physical space for purchasing additional fresh and salable merchandise. Selling obsolete goods is not a difficult process. Often a simple warehouse sale with advance promotions is all that is necessary.

It has been my experience that many owners attribute their cash problems to areas unrelated to inventory obsolescence. As a matter of fact, many owners believe that all inventory items tend to date quickly, especially in the area of fashions, for example. I have also found that many businesses have been based on the premise that a high and ample inventory stock linked to marketing policy requires quick turnover and rapid replacement. These types of businesses are the very ones that suffer and sometimes fail during an economic recession. Nonetheless, there are lessons to be learned from such circumstances.

To start with, buying merchandise for resale is an art subject to some risk. Second, once merchandise is purchased, it ought to be viewed as money that is being shelved as stock. Third, if you have to give it away at deeply discounted prices there is a desperate need for inventory controls and a revised marketing program. Even steps by a professional to sell obsolete merchandise are no more than a stop gap measure, and, to repeat, such a strategy is neither feasible nor profitable. Therefore, a carefully developed program of inventory control is your only step to permanent control.

Productivity

Of all the factors in business that can lead to success or failure, productivity is the one owners find difficult to understand and identify.

Productivity can be defined as the rate of worker's output within a given time frame and at a specified cost. Thus, increased productivity is the result of a greater output of goods

CASH, THE EQUALIZER   197

and services without a corresponding increase in cost. Gains
in output without cost increases means greater profits; lower
productivity increases the cost per item and eventually reduces existing cash reserves. Governments measure a nation's
overall productivity in terms of gross national product. The
accepted belief within the economic circle of government is
that increased productivity results in an increase in the gross
national product, which in turn contributes to a higher standard of living for all. Thus, the productivity of employees
has been a bone of contention between large corporations
and their union counterparts for years. Attempts by large
corporations to increase productivity through automation
have given unions problems with their rank and file, while
great productivity from foreign competitors has given U.S.
companies problems within their own management.

Over the years I have found that many small business owners
have a better understanding and control over productivity
than large corporations. I attribute this to the closer rapport
that exists between management and the workers in small
businesses. For large corporations, the luxury of individual
attention to the worker's needs is impossible. However, this
does not necessarily mean that all small to medium-sized
businesses maintain higher levels of productivity than larger
companies. Many business owners have never established
standards for their employees and face the same problems
in the level of output and the quality of worker performance
experienced by large-scale operations. Furthermore, the lack
of productivity in a smaller business can have a greater impact
on the smaller operation than the actions of a few employees
within a larger corporation.

The professional's first steps to resolve a problem in this area
is to review the whole operation for possible bottlenecks in
production, correct the obvious ones within the production
flow, and reduce the workforce where possible. Because of
the limited time often placed upon the professional to for-
mulate these assessments, judgment factors must be made
carefully but rapidly. For example, a deep cut in personnel
can result in a loss of output unless the duties of the employees released are reassigned to those remaining. In addition, bottlenecks in production can arise from reducing the

working force unless the work duties are properly reassigned and work stations equally balanced. Generally, this means reassigning work duties for an even flow of production. Nevertheless, it has been my experience that the most immediate effect of reducing the size of the workforce is to increase cash funds. Such programs as establishing work standards, increasing output against established standards, and training employees to do work efficiently will improve and ensure a continuous high level of productivity.

To enable you to better understand what a small business owner can save with better standards of work performance, let me describe the case history of just one such owner. His business was service-oriented, a cleaning service for commercial businesses. Prior to the establishment of job standards, his jobs were never finished on time. Customers complained about the delays, and if he pushed his workers too hard they usually quit in protest. Finally, he decided to set specific work standards for the employees to follow. In the beginning, he studied the different methods each of his employees followed in completing their cleaning efforts. No two workers approached the work in the same manner. Through observing and interviewing his employees he began to establish standard methods of operation. Methods that would result in the best job at the least cost were adopted as standards. The standards were applied to all workers. Those workers with the wrong approach were correctly retrained. The results of this effort were rewarding to the owner in many ways. More work was done in less time, enabling the owner to accept additional business with the same work force. Employees were happier working under the new methods. They could now complete their jobs sooner with fewer complaints from the boss. This was not a complex system, but benefits gained from its implementation more than justified the business owner's efforts.

Fixed and Variable Expenses

Although we have discussed the area of fixed and variable expenses rather extensively in previous chapters, some of the essentials are worth repeating.

The professional is usually called upon as a last resort to stop the continual drain on working capital. The professional must concentrate on two areas: stopping all expenditures both fixed and variable at their source and redirecting the payment of all existing liabilities over a beneficial period. Like other steps of last resort, these actions are initiated for immediate results to stop any further drain on existing cash reserves. But having long-range controls on both fixed and variable expenses where expenses are targeted at the source in correlation to long-term projections is the real key to maintaining a workable cash reserve for future operations.

Capital Expenditures

Many business owners confuse the acquisition of capital equipment as an expense reduction that ultimately reduces taxable profits along with cash funds. Capital expenditures for equipment and other tangible property are not deductible expense items and therefore should never appear on the business owner's profit and loss statements. Capital items can be depreciated over the anticipated life of the asset, and that is deductible from profits as a depreciation expense. However, this expense deduction is only a portion of the total capital expenditure.

This raises some serious questions about how one justifies the acquisition of any capital equipment, especially when the funds involved result in a reduction of cash but have no immediate effect on taxable profits. Briefly, it can be justified in several ways. Need, the increased productivity resulting from the acquisition, and the anticipated profit the acquisition of the capital investment can bring in the future are all sound reasons for capital expenditures.

There is a simple equation a small business owner can apply to determine whether or not a capital expenditure is wise. Assume that an owner pays $30,000 for a new piece of machinery. The new machine is acquired to replace an existing machine and will perform at twice the speed of the previous machine. The old machine produces approximately $20,000 worth of parts at cost each year. The trade-in allowance for the old machine is $5,000. The cost of the new machine is

$30,000, less the trade-in allowance of $5,000. Accelerated depreciation in the first year is taken at $5,000 and deducted from the cost. It is also known that production costs for parts for the old machine were $10,000 per year, and production costs for the new machine are estimated at $20,000 per year. From a cash standpoint, the new machine would pay back the owner at the end of the first year of operation. Of course, one can add other factors to the equation that will make it more complicated, such as investment credits, capital gains, increased worker's efficiency, and reduced maintenance costs—but the point is nonetheless well made.

If more small business owners justified their own capital expenditures in a similar way, there would be less need for professional assistance to rectify problems of overcapitalization. The first step for the professional is to complete an assessment of the return on investment for the existing equipment in a manner similar to the one described above. The final action will be to sell off both old and unused equipment along with equipment that offers little return on investment. In the meantime, in order to maintain current levels of production, the business owner may propose leading certain equipment on a temporary basis rather than purchasing new equipment. Once again, the focus is on securing cash as quickly as possible, but the long-term goal for the business owner remains to evaluate all capital acquisitions more carefully in terms of return.

A case in point is a machine shop operation that produced 85 percent of its products for the automobile industry. When the automotive market began to slow down and major customers stopped buying, 85 percent of his existing market vanished. By the time I was requested to assess the situation, the business was about ready to close its doors. With a mere 15 percent of the owner's original market remaining intact, he was still spending cash for fixed expenses, and no action had been taken to control variable expenses with the minor exception of terminating a few people on payroll. Working capital funds were being depleted with more money being disbursed than received. The owner had become a target for all sorts of wild financial schemes. He was offered sizable amounts of money on loan at ridiculous interest rates. Some former customers began to offer him subcontracting work below his cost because they knew how desperate he was to acquire business. Needless to add, his personal life suffered too. I instituted almost every step mentioned [here].

After four months of concentrated effort, I was able to stop further hemorrhaging of cash funds and begin to rebuild his organization. As you might suspect, one of my major efforts was to develop a new market for his operation. I targeted this new product market with lines designed to appeal to the automotive replacement parts market, having established that people were keeping their cars longer and needed parts for repair. After a review of this market and customer demands, it became apparent that the demand for repair parts in the automotive aftermarket was growing faster than the owner's demand for new automotive parts. Over the next two years I rebuilt his organization into a profitable operation at one-half its original size.

. . . I have concentrated on steps of last resort that a business owner should consider if his or her business is on the brink of failure. These steps are necessary only when a business has reached a point where the adoption of programs to keep a business healthy is no longer feasible. However, once a business has regained its former position of strength, the adoption of a permanent program to avoid bankruptcy is an absolute must for every business owner.*

There were many key factors that influenced our decision that the XYZ Company could not be saved from bankruptcy. Our major concern was prompted by the simple fact that there was not enough time to implement a program of this magnitude. The only individual who might have been able to operate the company once we had finished our assignment was Bob. After considerable deliberation among ourselves, the consensus was that Bob did not have enough experience to hold the XYZ Company together. Furthermore, we felt that he would be far better off to start fresh with his own smaller business from the remains of the XYZ Company and

*Excerpted, with permission, from Emery Toncré, *The Action-Step Plan to Avoiding Business Bankruptcy* (Englewood Cliffs, N.J.: Prentice-Hall, 1984), pp. 112—127.

to gain valuable experience as his business venture developed. As one of our last steps, the previous owners were contacted and refused to become involved. In short, there was no advantage for anyone in rebuilding the XYZ Company into a profitable operation. To be quite honest, the XYZ Company was beyond help.

On April 12, 1980, the XYZ Company filed for bankruptcy under Chapter 13. On April 13, 1980, the doors of XYZ Company were closed for the last time. As I stood across the street and watched the doors being padlocked, my mind continued to reflect on the same thought; in playing the game of economic survival, the XYZ Company had been dealt a stacked deck by its owners of monetary greed from the start. The combination of monetary greed and an attitude of total indifference to cash management can be lethal, and will most probably lead to business failure. As a result, XYZ never had a chance.

8

FUTURE TRENDS IN CASH MANAGEMENT

Within a few short years, there will be only two types of business owners: those who believe in the need for strong cash management controls, and those who continue to walk the thin line between success or failure, completely indifferent to cash flow.

Let me describe a case of a client in the second category, whose treatment of cash funds to avoid eventual failure was rather unique and in many ways quite clever. He was determined to make a success of his business, but his control over cash disbursements was nonexistent. As a result, one day he could be on the edge of failure and the next day flush with surplus funds. His self-styled spending spree was quite innovative. For example, in paying delinquent taxes he would attach different checks to different assessments, thereby causing as much confusion as possible when the IRS received his payment. In some cases, the amount he paid was greater than the initial tax assessment, which added more confusion as he attempted to distort the tax delinquency. His treatment of vendors was just as confusing. Invoices were purposely mixed with different checks which varied as to the correct amount. Vendors to whom he owed considerable money were asked for more supplies in order to complete work in process for customers who were expected to pay when the work was finished, on the promise that the vendors would be paid the total bill on completion of the job. This was usually enough inducement to get most vendors to go along with the scheme. Working in the field of construction permitted this owner to start one job, taking partial payment from the customer before completion and then using the money from the first job to begin a second job. If the customer complained about the work not being completed on time, he would simply say that he was temporarily short of supplies and needed an additional advance to complete the job. Most customers gave him the additional money rather than wait.

For this individual, the juggling of cash was a game—one that was often just short of being illegal—at which he was a master player. The adoption of this practice would put the average business owner out of business within four to six months. Furthermore, it is obviously not the basis for the cash management program I have detailed throughout the text, but for a simple game of chance.

As our fiscal policy within the business community continues to unfold over the coming years, I see no changes in the tight fiscal policies now plaguing the business community. Frankly, I believe the problems of cash shortages will continue to become an even greater problem over the coming year. Many factors are involved, but perhaps the most obvious contributors are the federal government and the growth of the national debt. As long as this debt continues to increase and as long as there is no serious attempt to restrain the government spending, government borrowing to pay interest on the present debt will be large enough to have a profound effect on the current money supply. The need for additional money in order to support the needs of our country, not to mention the loans to third world countries, along with worldwide competition that has made us a debtor nation, will continue to foster a government policy of deficit financing and place pressure on our existing money supply.

Given just this one fact, I firmly believe that more attention will have to be given by businesses to cash flow and disbursements practices than ever before. I am not alone in my belief that cash represents the bottom line for all business decisions and for business survival itself. In a recent book, Paul J. Beehler commented on trends on cash forecasting and set forth a detailed analysis of just one of the many cash forecasting models available today:

> Current developments indicate that cash forecasting today is in an evolutionary period between "indigenous" corporate internal forecasting methods and gradual adoption of more model-oriented methods. The basic movement in cash forecasting is in two areas: the media used to develop and control forecasts and the techniques that are used in making forecasts. These two factors are interrelated and affect the large corporations as well as intermediate-size firms.
>
> The delivery systems available to provide cash forecasts are now accelerating in development through time-sharing vendors. These services provide basic short-term forecasts (daily) for the corporation by duplicating a cash receipts and disbursements approach automatically for the corporation. This modus operandi is more advantageous than manual methods because it has the ability to extract data from other services such as automated deposit reporting services that are currently offered. Although there are quantitative techniques available through automated services, the potential use is only embryonic in its current manifestation. However, as a practical matter, short-term uses of quantitative techniques are limited because most firms have not experienced a demonstrated need for these techniques. There is a diminished trend within many corporations to develop internal forecasting models as flexible package forecasting models become available. Very large corporations, however, still develop internal models specifically to meet indigenous operating requirements.
>
> Within the next few years longer-term forecasts will also be increasingly provided by general purpose forecasting services offered by banks and time-sharing vendors. In this area, a wider use of quantitative modeling will occur because of user

operational ease. Liaison personnel from the supplier will work with the corporate cash manager to define forecast requirements and implement appropriate techniques for the corporation. Results will not always be optimal to the corporation, however, under this approach, but development and operational expenses will be minimal. Direct estimating of elements in the forecast will continue to be input by the corporation; however, the forecast of many elements will be based on various techniques. . . .

Specific applications will focus on dynamic forecasting of disbursement using time-sharing models. This use will be extended to forecasting of collections using daily inputs from corporate cash managers utilizing office resident computer terminals. Following a period of experimentation the outputs of both models will be merged into dynamic daily cash receipts and disbursement forecasting services.

Key elements in the development of a forecasting system involve (1) the selection of critical forecast variables, (2) the identification of forecast elements, (3) implementation of a data gathering system, and (4) the installation of a data updating and model-improvement system mechanism. The use of an adaptive controller for model improvement is the most critical element to achieving an acceptable forecast accuracy.*

As you can see, both Mr. Beehler's comments on the establishment of forecasting models for cash flow and automation and my discussion on the basic need for a cash management program emphasize the need for a sound cash management program. An effective cash management program will place complex problems in focus and permit the small business owner to make the proper decisions at the right time to assure sufficient working capital to operate his or her business.

Since cash represents the bottom line for making all decisions in business, the average business owner who adopts sound and constructive cash principles will become more

---

*Excerpted from Paul J. Beehler, *Contemporary Cash Management: Principles, Practices, Perspectives* (New York: Wiley, 1983), pp. 235–236.

proficient in business dealings with others. Cash planning, a procedure often ignored by business owners, has become the number one management tool for success. As more emphasis is placed on proper tax planning, antiquated accounting systems will eventually give way to more informative financial cash records. Simple maintenance of records of past performances will evolve into more modern cash systems that will tell you from a cash standpoint where you are today, and where you will be tomorrow.

Only those owners who understand how to utilize this cash control system will survive and be a part of tomorrow's business community.

INDEX